Summer Gatherings

Summer Gatherings

Casual Food to Enjoy with Family and Friends

Rick Rodgers

Photographs by Ben Fink

WM
WILLIAM MORROW
An Imprint of HarperCollinsPublishers

HarperCollins books may be purchased for educational, business, or sales promotional use. For information please write: Special Markets Department, HarperCollins Publishers, 10 East 53rd Street, New York, NY 10022.

FIRST EDITION

Designed by Lorie Pagnozzi

Library of Congress Cataloging-in-Publication Data has been applied for.

ISBN 978-0-06-143850-9

08   09   10   11   12   ID/RRD   10   9   8   7   6   5   4   3   2   1

To Steve, Cynthia, Ron, and Patrick,
and our summers in the mountains

Contents

Introduction

More and more, sharing a meal with friends and family has changed from an everyday occurrence to a less common affair. So when you do gather with loved ones, the event should be savored.

Any meal is just that more convivial when it takes place outside with the warm summer sun shining down on everyone involved. The self-appointed cook is happily ensconced at the grill, the kids are running around the yard letting off steam, and other folks are relaxing with a tall glass of iced tea.

Equinox dates do not a season make. At our house, summer is not just designated by dates, but by the food we eat from Memorial Day to Labor Day. During the course of the summer, the days are marked by when I first enjoy foods that I can only have in June, July, and August. The first buttered ear of corn, a beautifully juicy peach, basil with its distinctive spicy scent, a ripe homegrown tomato, a crunchy fried soft-shell crab, and more are all celebrated through my summertime cooking. I also have a mental checklist of particular summertime dishes—lobster rolls, grilled hamburgers and hot dogs with homemade condiments, fresh berry or peach pies—that I am sure to prepare before autumn chills the air.

Although my town is in a very densely populated suburban area, it is blessed with nearby farmland and a plethora of farmers' markets and farm stands. My menus are decided by what is in season locally and at the peak of its flavor. During the summer, I'll sometimes zero in on the expected tomatoes, herbs, summer squash, eggplants, berries, stone fruits, cucumbers, and the like. But just as often, I'll find myself face-to-face with something that I haven't cooked with in years, like gooseberries or currants. I've used them all in this book. I've also given some shopping tips on how to choose and prepare some of these fruits and vegetables.

Summer Gatherings offers recipes to cook for and with loved ones for both everyday meals and special occasions. Whether it is a holiday cookout, a kick-back brunch with weekend guests, or a weeknight supper, food has to get on the table. While it has always been my goal to provide tasty recipes with the most flavor for the least effort, summer is a particularly relaxed time when people don't want to spend a lot of time in a hot kitchen. These recipes are purposely casual in execution. Stripped to their essentials, they are uncomplicated by extraneous sauces or fussy garnishes. There are a couple of recipes for large gatherings that may take a bit more time (and can be prepared well ahead of serving), but in general, you'll average fifteen to thirty minutes of actual hands-on labor to make these dishes. Make-ahead and storage instructions are provided. Some cooks consider themselves nonbakers, but I guarantee you that the baked goods in this book can be made by novices with professional-tasting results.

It is a well-known tenet of cooking that your food will only be as good as your ingredients. The great news about summer cooking is that, with proper shopping, the produce is so delicious that you are already halfway there in creating a terrific meal. As I developed recipes for this book, time and again I was struck by the flavors of local, seasonal produce. Sure, you can buy peaches in February, but what are they going to taste like? Cooks are becoming increasingly aware of how the fuel used to transport produce around the world is impacting our environment, and of the efficiency of cooking with local ingredients. While this is not a book about sustainable agriculture, it is hoped that you will find cooking with food from your region's farms so flavorful that you will look for ways to buy local as much as possible.

So whether you are putting together a menu for a Father's Day backyard barbecue, a Fourth of July clambake, a graduation buffet, or a quick weeknight dinner, *Summer Gatherings* will help you create easy dishes that rejoice in the season's bounty.

APPETIZERS AND BEVERAGES

Apricots with Goat Cheese and Hazelnuts

Grilled Pizza with Corn, Monterey Jack, and Cilantro

White Peach Bellini Freezes

Heirloom Tomato and Cheese Tart

Quick Sweet and Sour Pickles

Fried Stuffed Zucchini Blossoms

Eggplant and Red Pepper Dip

Frozen Watermelon-Mint Daiquiris

Iced Tea-Ade

Apricots with Goat Cheese and Hazelnuts

My friend, cookbook author Linda Eckhardt, brought these to a cookout, and they disappeared. The combination of sweet apricot, tart goat cheese, and crunchy nuts is irresistible. If you wish, substitute pistachios (they don't need to be skinned) for the hazelnuts.

½ cup hazelnuts

9 ripe apricots

4 ounces rindless goat cheese, at room temperature

1. Position an oven rack in the center of the oven and preheat the oven to 350°F. Spread the hazelnuts on a baking sheet. Bake, stirring occasionally, until the hazelnut skins are cracked, about 12 minutes. Transfer the nuts to a clean kitchen towel and let cool until easy to handle. Using the towel as an aid, rub the skins off the hazelnuts (but do not worry about removing every trace of skin!). Cool completely. Coarsely chop the hazelnuts and place them in a shallow bowl.

2. Cut the apricots in half lengthwise and remove the pits. If desired, cut large apricots in half again. Spread the cut sides with the goat cheese. Press the goat-cheese side of each apricot into the hazelnuts to evenly coat the cheese. (The apricots can be prepared up to 4 hours ahead, covered, and refrigerated. Bring to room temperature before serving.) Arrange the apricots on a platter and serve.

Apricots

Apricots herald the arrival of early summer. It was just recently that my long aversion to these yellow-orange fruits was finally broken. When I was growing up, our backyard in California was shaded by a large, prolific apricot tree. No matter how sweet the fruit, nor how beautiful the tree was in bloom, I hated apricots. One of my household chores was cutting the lawn, and the many sticky orbs that dropped from the tree got in the way of my job. Now that a few years have passed, I have finally let go of my prejudice.

The best apricots have a honeylike sweetness. And they are good for you, high in fiber, beta carotene, and vitamin A. Apricots should be chosen as for peaches. Look for fragrant fruit that barely yields to the touch, and let them ripen, if necessary, at room temperature. Their skins are thin, and you rarely have to peel them for cooking. Almost all commercial apricots are grown in California, but because early picking makes for less tasty fruit, it is best to search out a local source where the fruit may be tree-ripened. I can buy Red Jacket apricots in New York State, and they are treasures.

Grilled Pizza with Corn, Monterey Jack, and Cilantro

Makes one 12-inch pizza, 4 appetizer servings

Grilled pizza was developed by George Germon and Johanne Killeen at Al Forno Restaurant in Providence about twenty years ago. At first, no dish seemed stranger, and now it is a national institution. This is a cross-cultural pizza with Mexican flavors, but it is a happy marriage. While you could make a couple of pizzas to serve as a main course, I find it more efficient to make a single pizza as an appetizer, accompanied by ice-cold beers or margaritas.

2 tablespoons extra virgin olive oil

1 garlic clove, crushed through a press

All-purpose flour, for the dough and pan

One 15-ounce package pizza dough, at room temperature

1⅓ cups (about 5 ounces) shredded Monterey Jack, divided

½ cup cooked corn kernels (cut from about 2 ears boiled or grilled corn)

1 scallion, white and green parts, finely chopped

1 poblano chile, roasted (see page 7), peeled, seeded, and coarsely chopped

2 tablespoons chopped fresh cilantro

1 lime, cut into wedges

1. Build a fire in an outdoor grill. For a charcoal grill, let the fire burn until the coals are covered with white ash, then let them burn for about 30 minutes until they are medium-hot (you should be able to hold your hand at the cooking grate level for 3 to 4 seconds). For a gas grill, preheat on high, then reduce the heat to medium.

2. Combine the oil and garlic in a small bowl and set aside.

3. Dust a rimless baking sheet with flour. On a lightly floured work surface, roll, pat, and stretch the dough into a 12-inch round. Transfer the round to the baking sheet and cover with plastic wrap.

4. Lightly oil the grill. Remove the plastic, slide the round of dough onto the grill, and cover. Grill until the underside is lightly toasted, about 3 minutes. Turn the dough. Leaving a 1-inch-wide border, sprinkle the round with ⅔ cup cheese, the corn, scallion, and chile. Top with the remaining ⅔ cup cheese. Brush the exposed dough border with some of the garlic oil. Cover and grill until the underside is toasted and the cheese is melted, about 3 minutes more.

5. Remove from the grill and drizzle with the remaining garlic oil. Sprinkle with the cilantro and cut into thin wedges. Serve hot, with the lime wedges passed for squeezing a few drops of juice over the pizza just before eating.

Peeling Chiles

Large chiles, such as poblanos, have thin but tough skins that are usually removed to render the chiles more tender. Roasting the chile chars the skin so it can be peeled off. To use a grill, build a hot fire in a charcoal or gas grill. Place the chiles on the grill and cover with the lid. Grill, turning occasionally, until the chiles are just charred and blistered on all sides, taking care not to burn a hole through the flesh, about 8 minutes. Or place the chiles on a broiler rack in a preheated broiler about 6 inches from the source of heat, turning occasionally. Transfer the chiles to a plate. Some recipes ask you to cover the chiles to create steam to loosen the skins. However, it also makes the chiles cool more slowly and increases the chance of overcooking them, so I let them cool uncovered. When they are cool enough to handle, remove the blackened skin, seeds, and stem. Coarsely chop the chiles and set aside.

If you are proceeding from grilling the chiles to grilling the pizza, let the coals in a charcoal grill burn down to medium-hot, or reduce the heat in a gas grill to medium.

White Peach Bellini Freezes

The Bellini, a sparkling wine and peach puree cocktail, traveled to America from Venice, where it supposedly originated at the famous Harry's Bar. There's just one problem: it can quickly lose its chill in the warm sun. The problem is solved by freezing the peach puree into granita, which, added to the wine, keeps the fizzy libation ice-cold. Serve it as a cocktail or, as I often do, as a dessert for brunch.

6 ripe white peaches

½ cup sugar

1 tablespoon fresh lemon juice

6 teaspoons red raspberry liqueur, such as Chambord

One 750-ml bottle sparkling wine, such as Prosecco, chilled

Peach slices, raspberries, and fresh mint sprigs, for garnish

1. Place a 9-inch diameter metal cake pan in the freezer to chill while preparing the peaches.

2. Bring a large saucepan of water to a boil over high heat. Place a large bowl of ice water next to the stove. Add the peaches to the boiling water and cook just until their skins loosen, about 30 seconds. Using a slotted spoon, transfer the peaches to the ice water and let stand until cooled. Drain the peaches. Peel, pit, and coarsely chop the peaches.

3. In a food processor fitted with the metal chopping blade (or in a blender, working in batches), combine the peaches, sugar, and lemon juice and process until pureed. Pour into the chilled cake pan. Freeze until the edges of the puree are icy, about 2 hours. Using a metal spoon, stir the puree to combine the icy and unfrozen parts together. Freeze until the edges are icy again, about 1 hour more. Repeat the stirring, and freeze until the puree is slushy, about 1 hour more. (The frozen peach slush can be covered and frozen for up to 1 day.)

4. Scoop equal amounts of the slush into 6 champagne flutes. Top each with 1 teaspoon raspberry liqueur. Slowly pour the sparkling wine into the flutes (you may have to nudge the peach slush with a long spoon to be sure that the wine reaches the bottom of the glass). Garnish each with a peach slice, raspberries, and a mint sprig and serve chilled, with long spoons to eat the slush, if you wish.

A Relaxed Breakfast with Friends

Corn Hotcakes with Blackberry Syrup (page 89)

Grilled Sausage and/or Fresh Cooked Bacon

Hot Coffee or Tea

White Peach Bellini Freezes (page 9)

Heirloom Tomato and Cheese Tart

Not only is this free-form phyllo tart colorful and tasty, it is also versatile. Cut it into small rectangles to serve as an appetizer with drinks, or place larger pieces atop a green salad as a first course. For the most dramatic effect, use a variety of not-too-big colored tomatoes; large tomatoes won't fill the crust as nicely as small ones.

6 small to medium heirloom tomatoes

12 sheets frozen phyllo dough, defrosted

1/4 cup extra virgin olive oil

2 tablespoons freshly grated Parmesan

2 ounces rindless goat cheese, crumbled

Salt and freshly ground black pepper

2 tablespoons finely chopped fresh herbs,
    such as a combination of basil, chives, and parsley

1. Position an oven rack in the center of the oven and preheat the oven to 375°F. Line a baking sheet with parchment paper.

2. Core and slice the tomatoes into 1/8- to 1/4-inch-thick rounds, discarding the end slices. (The tomatoes should be cut on the thin side so their juices can evaporate during baking before they have a chance to make the crust soggy.) Place the tomato rounds on paper towels. Cover with another layer of paper towels and let stand to drain excess juices while preparing the phyllo crust.

3. Place a phyllo sheet on the baking sheet. Brush the phyllo with olive oil. Top with the remaining phyllo sheets, brushing each with oil. Fold over the four sides of the phyllo stack to make a ¾-inch-wide border. Sprinkle the area inside the border with the Parmesan. Top with the tomato slices, overlapping the slices as needed. Sprinkle with the goat cheese and season with salt and pepper to taste.

4. Bake until the phyllo is crisp and deep golden brown, about 20 minutes. Cool slightly or to room temperature. Sprinkle with the herbs, cut into rectangles, and serve.

Heirloom Tomatoes

Fire-truck-red, baseball-size tomatoes are a familiar sight, and you can buy a tomato in the dead of winter, if you want to. But in the last few years, tomatoes have broken through the color barrier, and when the summer tomato season reaches fever pitch, you'll see yellow, orange, green, and striped tomatoes along with many different shades of red, from burgundy to pink.

Instead of the usual "modern" commercial hybrids, these tomatoes are grown from old varieties. They are often called "heirloom" to indicate that they come from antique strains. These tomatoes are grown for flavor, not for ease of shipping. Some of them may seem misshapen and downright ugly—until tasted and then you realize that looks aren't everything. Just cut away the gnarly parts and savor what's left. Few dishes signal summer cooking more than a platter of sliced heirloom tomatoes of different hues, simply dressed with olive oil, a sprinkle of sea salt, and perhaps some torn basil leaves.

Quick Sweet
and Sour Pickles

Putting up pickles can be a pleasure, but most of us don't have the room for storage nor the large family to eat them up by the next summer. Therefore, I make my pickles one jar at a time. They will get a bit soggy after a week or two, but the pickles don't stay uneaten for longer than that.

4 Kirby cucumbers, scrubbed, cut lengthwise into quarters

3 teaspoons fine sea salt, divided

2 cups white distilled vinegar

2/3 cup sugar

1/2 teaspoon yellow mustard seed

1/4 teaspoon whole allspice

1/4 teaspoon black peppercorns

2 whole cloves

1. Toss the cucumbers with 1 1/2 teaspoons of the salt in a medium bowl. Add 4 cups ice cubes and mix gently. Let stand for 1 hour. Drain in a colander and rinse the cucumbers under cold running water. Drain again and pat dry with paper towels.

2. Bring the vinegar, sugar, remaining 1 1/2 teaspoons salt, mustard seed, allspice, peppercorns, and cloves to a boil in a nonreactive saucepan over medium heat, stirring to dissolve the sugar.

3. Place the cucumbers upright in a hot, clean 1-quart canning jar. Pour the hot vinegar mixture into the jar and close the jar with the lid. Let cool to tepid. Refrigerate overnight. (The pickles can be refrigerated for up to 2 weeks.) To serve, remove the pickles from the liquid.

Cucumbers

Crisp and refreshing, cucumbers are endlessly useful in summer cooking, making many appearances in chilled soups and salads. There are more cucumbers to consider than the ubiquitous shiny, dark green, waxed and long, English seedless varieties. Kirby cucumbers, a nubbly pale green, have a crunchy texture that makes them perfect for pickling. Long, curved Persian cucumbers are becoming more common at farmers' markets. Neither of these varieties needs peeling—just scrub them with a vegetable brush.

Cucumbers have two characteristics that cooks have to address: seeds and water. The seeds can be tough and are often removed. To remove cucumber seeds, slice the cucumber lengthwise and scoop out the seeds with the tip of a dessertspoon.

In marinated salads, cucumbers will give off plenty of liquid and dilute the dressing, so it is a good idea to remove excess juices. Toss the cut cucumbers with a sprinkle of salt, and let stand in a colander for an hour or so. Rinse under cold running water to remove excess salt. When seasoning, keep in mind that the cucumber will have absorbed some salt flavor, so be judicious.

Fried Stuffed Zucchini Blossoms

Makes 16 blossoms

Harvesting zucchini blossoms is a great way of controlling the amount of summer squash in the garden, and my local farm stands always have piles of them for sale. I usually pass them over, but then, in the same week, two friends of mine, Barbara Caccavella and Marguerite Scandiffio, separately rhapsodized about how their Italian-American families fried up piles of blossoms every summer. To avoid deep-frying indoors over a hot stove, fry them in batches in an electric skillet outdoors and serve them, hot and crisp, right out of the pan.

BATTER

1 cup all-purpose flour

¼ teaspoon salt

1¼ cups club soda, as needed

16 zucchini blossoms

½ cup ricotta

4 teaspoons finely chopped fresh basil

1 garlic clove, crushed through a press

Salt and freshly ground black pepper

Vegetable oil, for deep-frying

1. To make the batter, using a fork, stir the flour and salt in a bowl to combine. Gradually whisk in the club soda to make a batter—there should be a few lumps of flour. Let stand 10 minutes to thicken slightly.

2. Using a small knife, cut a slit down the side of each zucchini blossom, and remove the pistil from inside each blossom. (If a blossom tears, don't worry.) Mix the ricotta, basil, and garlic in a small bowl and season with salt and pepper to taste. Using a small spoon (a demitasse spoon works well), insert a heaping spoonful of the ricotta mixture inside each blossom through the slit. Be sure that the cheese filling is completely enclosed by the blossom. Transfer the blossoms to a platter.

3. Place a wire cake rack on a rimmed baking sheet. Pour enough oil into a large skillet to come halfway up the sides. Heat over high heat until the oil reaches 360°F on a deep-frying thermometer. One at a time, holding the blossom by the stem, dip the blossom into the batter and remove, letting excess batter drip back into the bowl. There should be only a light coating of batter. Place in the oil and fry, turning once, until golden brown, about 2 minutes. Fry the blossoms in batches to avoid crowding them in the skillet. Using a wire skimmer, transfer the blossoms to the cake rack to drain. Serve hot.

Eggplant and Red Pepper Dip

There is something almost comical in how a big, balloonlike eggplant deflates during grilling. But there's nothing funny about the taste, as the flesh becomes tender with a smoky flavor. Grill a red pepper along with the eggplant and combine the two to make a winning dip, perfect for spreading on baguette slices or toasted pita wedges.

2 purple eggplants, about 1 pound each

1 large red bell pepper, cut open, seeds and ribs removed, and prepared for roasting (see page 66)

1 garlic clove

¼ cup plain yogurt

2 tablespoons chopped fresh basil

Salt and freshly ground black pepper

Baguette slices or toasted pita wedges, for serving

1. Build a hot fire in a charcoal or gas grill. Place the eggplants and red pepper, skin side down, on the grill and cover.

   Red pepper: Grill, without turning, until the skin is blackened and blistered, about 8 minutes. Transfer to a plate and cool. Peel off and discard the skin.
   Eggplant: Grill, turning occasionally, until the eggplant skin is blackened on all sides and the eggplant collapses, about 20 minutes. Transfer to a plate and cool. Scrape the tender flesh from the skin into a bowl and discard the skin.

2. With the machine running, drop the garlic through the feed tube of a food processor fitted with the metal chopping blade to finely chop the garlic. Add the eggplant flesh, red pepper, yogurt, and basil. Pulse until the mixture is coarsely chopped. Season with salt and pepper to taste. (The dip can be covered and refrigerated for up to 3 days.) Transfer to a serving bowl and serve with the bread.

Frozen Watermelon-Mint Daiquiris

Makes 1½ cups mint syrup, 4 to 6 drinks

Sipping a frosty frozen daiquiri is one of the benefits of being an adult in the summertime. This watermelon version uses homemade mint syrup as an ingredient, which will come in handy when you want to sweeten iced teas or other beverages (it will make a fabulous mint julep). This has become our house summer cocktail, and I always have refrigerated mint syrup and frozen watermelon chunks at the ready.

MINT SYRUP

1 cup sugar

1 cup packed fresh mint leaves

4 cups (1-inch cubes) seedless watermelon

1 cup silver rum

½ cup Mint Syrup

½ cup fresh lime juice

Fresh mint sprigs, for garnish

1. To make the syrup, combine 1 cup water, the sugar, and the mint in a medium saucepan. Bring to a boil over medium heat, stirring often to dissolve the sugar. Remove from the heat and let cool completely. Strain through a wire sieve into a jar, pressing hard on the mint leaves with a wooden spoon. (The mint syrup can be stored in a jar and refrigerated for up to 2 months.)

2. Spread the watermelon on a rimmed baking sheet. Freeze until the watermelon is solid, about 3 hours. (The watermelon chunks can be stored in a self-locking plastic bag and frozen for up to 1 month.)

3. In two batches, combine the watermelon, rum, syrup, and lime juice in a blender and process until smooth. Pour into glasses and garnish with mint sprigs. Serve chilled.

Watermelon

Watermelon may be enjoyed as a fruit, but it is actually closely related to pumpkin and other squashes. For most of us, our memories of summers past include chomping away at a huge, sweet, and sticky wedge of watermelon, and spitting the seeds at whatever kid was unlucky enough to be nearby (it didn't have to be a sibling, but it helped).

If current trends hold, the big watermelon riddled with seeds will become a thing of the past. Small "individual" seedless melons (actually, the seeds are there, just very thin and almost invisible), some with yellow, and not red, flesh, are flooding the market. The new melons are very tasty and, if they are harvested correctly, the flavor difference between the new and old varieties is hard to detect.

In any case, choose your watermelons by looks (the underbelly should be pale yellow, indicating that it ripened while on the ground, and not white) or by the thump test (rap your finger against the melon and listen for a deep resonant sound).

Iced Tea-Ade

Although this recipe is so simple that it may not warrant writing down, it bows to the popularity of two summer thirst-quenchers, iced tea and lemonade. Whenever I serve it to my guests, I get compliments, which must point to how accustomed people have become to stirring up instant beverages instead of taking a few minutes to make the superior homemade versions. If you purchase an inexpensive electric fruit juicer, you could find yourself making this drink at every opportunity.

6 orange pekoe tea bags

½ cup fresh lemon juice

⅔ cup superfine sugar
   (or process granulated sugar in a blender until finely ground)

Fresh mint sprigs, for garnish (optional)

1. Combine the tea bags with 1 quart water in a large pitcher. Let stand (in the sunlight, if you wish) until the tea is steeped, at least 2 and up to 8 hours. Remove the bags from the pitcher, squeezing the bags to release as much brewed tea as possible.

2. Stir the lemon juice and sugar in a bowl to dissolve the sugar. Stir in 1 quart cold water. Stir into the brewed tea. (The tea-ade can be refrigerated for up to 5 days.) Serve over ice, garnished with a mint sprig, if desired.

SOUPS AND SALADS

Summer Minestrone

Squash Blossom Soup with Corn and Zucchini Salsa

Chilled Vegetarian Borscht

Layered Salad with Creamy Sweet Onion Dressing

Watermelon, Tomato, and Mint Salad

Arugula, Prosciutto, and Cantaloupe Salad

Gazpacho-Style Bread Salad

Classic Basil Pesto

Potato Salad with Green Beans and Pesto

Grilled Corn and Bean Salad with Chile Vinaigrette

Grilled Vegetable Salad with Tomato Vinaigrette

Summer Minestrone

Makes 6 to 8 servings

The first time I had this refreshing soup was at an outdoor trattoria in Florence. After a morning of walking in the summer heat, I wanted a light meal, so I ordered minestrone, but I didn't expect it to be cool. It was a revelation and you may prefer it to the hot version, as I do. Made with farm-fresh vegetables, it is simply wonderful and a great way to use summer's bounty.

2 tablespoons extra virgin olive oil

1 medium onion, chopped

½ red bell pepper, seeds and ribs removed, cut into ¼-inch dice

1 garlic clove, finely chopped

2 small zucchini, scrubbed and cut into ½-inch dice

½ pound green beans, cut into ½-inch lengths

1 pound shelled fresh cranberry beans (1 cup shelled beans)

6 cups vegetable stock (see page 35)

1 large ripe tomato, seeded and cut into ½-inch dice

¼ teaspoon chopped fresh thyme

½ cup rice for risotto, such as Arborio (see Note)

Salt and freshly ground black pepper

Chopped fresh basil, for garnish

1. Heat the oil in a soup pot over medium heat. Add the onion and red pepper and cook, stirring occasionally, until softened, about 3 minutes. Stir in the garlic and cook until it gives off its aroma, about 1 minute longer. Stir in the zucchini, green beans, and cranberry beans.

2. Add the stock, 2 cups water, tomato, and thyme, and bring to a boil over high heat. Reduce the heat to low and partially cover the pot. Simmer until the vegetables are tender, about 30 minutes.

3. Meanwhile, bring a medium saucepan of lightly salted water to a boil over high heat. Add the rice and reduce the heat to medium. Cook at a brisk simmer until the rice is tender, about 18 minutes. Drain the rice in a wire sieve and rinse under cold running water.

4. When the vegetables are tender, stir the rice into the soup and cook for a few minutes to blend the flavors. Season with salt and pepper to taste. Cool to room temperature. (The soup can be cooled, covered, and refrigerated for up to 3 days. Remove from the refrigerator at least 1 hour before serving.) Serve at room temperature, sprinkled with the basil.

Note

A couple of tips about the Arborio rice in this soup. Resist the temptation to add the rice uncooked directly to the soup: it will soak up too much of the broth, and you'll end up with porridge instead of soup. And serve the soup at room temperature, not chilled, as cold rice has an unpleasant, pelletlike texture.

Squash Blossom Soup with Corn and Zucchini Salsa

Makes 6 to 8 servings

It turns out that Italian cooks aren't the only ones who appreciate squash blossoms. My friend Priscila Satakoff, chef/owner of Chicago's Salpicón restaurant, once told me that she knew Mexican cooking had arrived in America when she could find squash blossoms at her market. She went on to say that her favorite way to cook them was in a soup, so I went into the kitchen and created this in her honor.

CORN AND ZUCCHINI SALSA

1 small zucchini, cut into ¼-inch dice

1 tomato, seeded and cut into ½-inch dice

½ teaspoon salt, plus more to taste

¾ cup fresh corn kernels (cut from 1 large ear corn)

3 tablespoons finely chopped red onion

½ jalapeño chile, finely chopped

2 tablespoons chopped fresh cilantro or basil

ZUCCHINI BLOSSOM SOUP

20 zucchini blossoms

2 tablespoons extra virgin olive oil

1 onion, chopped

2 garlic cloves, finely chopped

4½ cups chicken broth, preferably homemade, or use low-sodium canned broth

¼ cup yellow cornmeal

Salt and freshly ground black pepper

Lime wedges, for serving

1. To make the salsa, toss the zucchini, tomato, and salt in a wire sieve and let stand to drain off excess juices, about 1 hour. Drain and pat dry with paper towels. Transfer to a bowl, add the corn, red onion, jalapeño, and cilantro, and mix gently. Season with salt. (The salsa can be prepared up to 4 hours ahead, covered, and stored at room temperature.)

2. To make the soup, trim the zucchini blossoms, leaving 2 to 3 inches of stem on each blossom. Cut off and coarsely chop the tender petals and inner blossom parts and set aside. Coarsely chop the stems and remaining parts; set aside.

3. Heat the oil in a soup pot over medium heat. Add the onion and cover. Cook, stirring occasionally, until tender, about 5 minutes. Stir in the reserved harder parts of the blossoms and the garlic. Cook, uncovered, until the garlic gives off its aroma, about 1 minute. Stir in the broth and bring to a boil over high heat. Reduce the heat to low and partially cover the pot. Simmer to blend the flavors, about 20 minutes.

4. Whisk the cornmeal and ½ cup water in a bowl. Stir into the soup, along with the reserved petals and tender parts of the blossoms. Cook until the soup is lightly thickened, about 10 minutes. Season with salt and pepper to taste.

5. Ladle the soup into bowls. Add a generous spoonful of the salsa to each bowl and serve with lime wedges.

Zucchini Blossoms

Wherever there are summer squash growing, there are squash blossoms. Some farmers are thrilled to find a market for the blossoms, because removing them from the vine controls the amount of squash that has to be harvested. Even for commercial farmers, there is such a thing as too many zucchini.

Don't expect to be bowled over by their flavor, which is faintly zucchinilike. Instead, appreciate them as a foil for a cheese stuffing and a crispy batter, or for the golden color they bring to soup. They are highly perishable, so don't buy more than you can use in a day or so, and keep them refrigerated. When preparing them for cooking, watch out for bees, which love to hide in the blossom's folds. I ignored this advice and was almost stung the last time I fried up some blossoms. Trim away the stems, leaving a 2-inch length to act as a handle.

To prepare squash blossoms for stuffing, make a slit through the side of the blossom and remove the pistil or stamen (which is edible, but not very tender). If the blossom splits open, don't worry—the petals will adhere to the filling and the blossom will hold its shape when battered and fried. And if you don't feel like stuffing the blossoms, just batter and fry them for a wonderful snack with a cool glass of white wine.

Chilled Vegetarian Borscht

Makes 6 to 8 servings

There are actually two kinds of borscht, hot and cold, and while both begin with beets, they are two very different recipes. Hot borscht usually includes meat and should not be chilled, as the fat hardens and is not very nice to eat. For the chilled version, a meatless recipe with vegetable stock is in order. Kohlrabi or celery root will add substance to the soup, and both taste much better than cold potatoes.

VEGETABLE STOCK

2 tablespoons vegetable oil

1 onion, chopped

2 carrots, chopped

2 celery ribs, chopped

6 garlic cloves, crushed under a knife and peeled

4 parsley sprigs

1/4 teaspoon dried thyme

1/4 teaspoon black peppercorns

1 bay leaf

2 tablespoons vegetable oil

1 onion, chopped

2 carrots, chopped

2 celery ribs, chopped

1 garlic clove, chopped

1 pound red beets, peeled and cut into 1/2-inch dice

1 medium kohlrabi or celery root (celeriac), peeled and cut into ½-inch dice

1 large beefsteak tomato, seeded and cut into ½-inch dice

3 tablespoons cider vinegar

2 tablespoons sugar

Salt and freshly ground black pepper

Sour cream, for serving

Chopped fresh dill, for serving

1. To make the stock, heat the oil in a large saucepan over medium heat. Add the onion, carrots, and celery and cover. Cook, stirring occasionally, until the onion is tender but not browned, about 6 minutes. Add the garlic and cook, uncovered, until it is fragrant, about 1 minute. Add 2½ quarts water, the parsley, thyme, peppercorns, and bay leaf. Cover and bring to a boil over high heat. Reduce the heat to medium and set the lid askew. Cook at a brisk simmer until reduced to 6 cups, about 40 minutes. Strain in a colander into a bowl, pressing hard on the solids. Set the stock aside.

2. To make the soup, heat the oil in a soup pot over medium heat. Add the onion, carrots, and celery. Cook, uncovered, stirring occasionally, until the onion is golden, about 5 minutes. Add the garlic and cook until it is fragrant, about 1 minute. Add the reserved stock, beets, kohlrabi, tomato, vinegar, and sugar, and bring to a boil. Reduce the heat to medium-low and partially cover the pot. Cook until the beets are tender, about 45 minutes. Season with salt and pepper to taste. Transfer to a bowl and cool to room temperature.

3. Cover and refrigerate until chilled, at least 4 hours or overnight. Reseason with salt and pepper. Serve the borscht chilled, topping each serving with a dollop of sour cream and a generous sprinkling of dill.

Layered Salad with Creamy Sweet Onion Dressing

Makes 8 servings

You can always rely on a fresh green salad made with seasonal vegetables to be a hit at an outdoor meal. Have fun by adding your favorite produce—the only constants in this layered salad are crisp (not tender) lettuce and a protective layer of cheese topped with a thick, creamy dressing. Sliced onions, garbanzo beans, fresh corn kernels, and cooked asparagus spears are all options.

DRESSING

1 cup mayonnaise

½ cup buttermilk (shake well before using)

1 small sweet onion, such as Vidalia, Maui, or Walla Walla, shredded on the large holes of a box grater

½ teaspoon celery seed

Salt and freshly ground black pepper

8 ounces green beans, trimmed and cut into 1-inch lengths

2 Kirby cucumbers, scrubbed, cut into ¼-inch-thick half-moons

1 head iceberg lettuce or 2 romaine hearts, torn into bite-sized pieces

1 pint cherry tomatoes

1 cup (4 ounces) crumbled blue cheese

1. To make the dressing, whisk the mayonnaise, buttermilk, grated onion, and celery seed in a medium bowl to combine. Season with salt and pepper to taste.

2. Bring a large saucepan of lightly salted water to a boil over high heat. Add the green beans and cook until crisp-tender, about 4 minutes. Drain, rinse under cold water, and drain again well. Pat dry with paper towels.

3. Place the green beans and cucumbers in a very large serving bowl. Top with the lettuce, then the cherry tomatoes. Sprinkle the blue cheese over the tomatoes. Spread the dressing over the cheese layer. (The salad can be made, covered tightly with plastic wrap, and refrigerated for up to 8 hours.)

4. Just before serving, toss the salad. Serve chilled.

Sweet Onions

Look closely at the labels of onions in the supermarket. Many imported onions (why onions have to fly around the world to get to my market is beyond me when domestic ones store so well) are now labeled "sweet," which I guess is supposed to be a benefit. Actually, cooking onions are supposed to be sharp, as they get sweeter when cooked. Cook a sweet onion and you get very little flavor.

But sweet onions are deliciously mellow in salads. There are many American sweet onions grown regionally; the variety is usually named for the locality in which the onion is grown. Look for Vidalia (Georgia), Maui (Hawaii), or Walla Walla (Washington) onions to add crunch to your salads.

Watermelon, Tomato, and Mint Salad

Makes 4 to 6 servings

What may seem like an incongruous mixture is actually a harmonious blend of ingredients and textures. There are few dishes that illustrate how the seemingly disparate flavors of sweet, sour, bitter, and salty can be successfully combined. Enjoy this salad as a cool first course, or as a side salad to simply grilled meats, especially lamb. One tip: while the melon should be chilled, the other ingredients are at their most flavorful at room temperature, so combine the salad just before serving.

½ small ("individual size") watermelon, preferably seedless

2 large ripe tomatoes, preferably green or orange heirlooms,
    seeded and cut into 1-inch cubes

1 small sweet onion, such as Vidalia, Maui, or Walla Walla, thinly sliced

2 tablespoons chopped fresh mint

½ cup (2 ounces) crumbled feta

1. Cut off and discard the watermelon rind. Cut the watermelon into 1-inch cubes, removing any seeds as needed. Transfer to a serving bowl. Cover and refrigerate until chilled, at least 1 hour and up to 12 hours.

2. Add the tomatoes, onion, and mint to the watermelon and toss gently. Add the feta cheese and toss again. Serve immediately.

Arugula, Prosciutto, and Cantaloupe Salad

Makes 6 to 8 servings

Cantaloupe and melon is a timeless, simple first course, and the addition of bracing arugula gives it a bit more substance. If you have access to imported Italian prosciutto di Parma, which is more delicate and less salty than the domestic version, use it here for a real treat. Regardless of the prosciutto you use, impress upon your delicatessen *not* to slice it paper-thin, or it will be too difficult to slice into ribbons for the salad.

2 tablespoons balsamic vinegar

½ cup extra virgin olive oil

Salt and freshly ground black pepper

1 small ripe cantaloupe

8 cups packed arugula leaves

4 ounces thinly sliced prosciutto (a little less than ¹/₁₆ inch thick)

1. Put the vinegar in a small bowl. Gradually whisk in the oil. Season with salt and pepper to taste. (The dressing can be made 1 day ahead, covered, and stored at room temperature.)

2. Cut the cantaloupe in half, and save one half for another use. Peel the cantaloupe and scoop out the seeds. Cut into ⅛-inch-thick slices, then cut each slice crosswise into thirds. Refrigerate until ready to serve.

3. Toss the arugula and vinaigrette in a large serving bowl. Add the cantaloupe and toss lightly. Cut the prosciutto (including the fat) into ⅛-inch-wide strips. Scatter over the top of the salad and toss again. Season with pepper and serve immediately.

Gazpacho-Style Bread Salad

Makes 6 servings

If someone ever takes a tally of the Best Summer Dishes, gazpacho will certainly be at the top of the list. There are many different manifestations of this cold soup—some are chunky, some are thin, and some don't even have any tomatoes. More often than not, I start by serving the dressed cubed tomato, cucumber, and sweet peppers as a salad topped with bread cubes. The next day, I whirl the leftovers in a food processor to make soup.

1 large cucumber, peeled, halved lengthwise, seeds removed with the tip of a spoon, and cut into $\frac{1}{2}$-inch dice

3 large ripe beefsteak tomatoes, seeds removed, cut into $\frac{3}{4}$-inch dice

$\frac{1}{2}$ teaspoon salt, plus more to taste

2 tablespoons sherry or red wine vinegar

1 garlic clove, crushed through a press

$\frac{1}{2}$ cup extra virgin olive oil

2 Italian frying (Cubanelle) peppers or 1 green bell pepper, seeds and ribs removed, chopped into $\frac{1}{2}$-inch dice

2 scallions, white and green parts, finely chopped

Freshly ground black pepper

2 cups ($\frac{3}{4}$-inch) day-old crusty, rustic bread cubes

1. Toss the cucumber, tomatoes, and salt together in a colander. Let stand in the sink to drain off excess juices, about 1 hour.

2. Whisk the vinegar and garlic in a large bowl. Gradually whisk in the oil. Add the cucumbers and tomatoes, peppers, and scallions. Mix gently and season with the pepper. Cover and refrigerate until the salad is chilled, at least 2 and up to 4 hours.

3. Just before serving, gently stir in the bread cubes and adjust the seasoning with salt and pepper. Serve chilled, using a slotted spoon.

Note

Gazpacho: Any leftover salad can be turned into a chilled gazpacho soup. The salad gives off a good amount of juices as it stands, so blending it into a soup is actually a better solution than serving soggy salad. Just process the salad—vegetables, bread, juices, and all—in a food processor or blender until it is as smooth as you like. If necessary, add some canned tomato juice or extra virgin olive oil to the salad as it is processed to adjust the consistency. Don't bother to remove the juice-soaked bread cubes from the salad, as they will blend smoothly into the soup and, in fact, give it some body, a trick that more than one Spanish cook has shared with me.

Classic Basil Pesto

Makes about 2 cups

Pesto is so much more than a pasta sauce. Make it all summer long, and add unrestrained dollops of the aromatic paste to salads, soups, tomato sauce, mayonnaise, and more. Here's a detailed recipe to share the tips I've learned over the years about how to make and store this indispensable seasonal treasure. The main idea here is to improvise (within reason), and use whatever nuts or hard grating cheese you have on hand. And don't overlook the peppery arugula variation, which is almost as useful as the basil classic.

2 garlic cloves, crushed under a knife and peeled

1/3 cup pine nuts, walnuts, or almonds

1/2 cup (2 ounces) freshly grated Parmesan or Romano, or a combination

3 cups packed fresh basil leaves, well rinsed and dried in a salad spinner

1/2 cup extra virgin olive oil, plus more to cover the pesto

Salt and freshly ground black pepper

1. With the machine running, drop the garlic through the feed tube of a food processor. Add the nuts and cheese, and process until the nuts are finely chopped. Add the basil. With the machine running, gradually add the oil, scraping down the sides of the work bowl as needed, to make a thick paste. Season with salt and pepper to taste.

2. Transfer the pesto to a shallow container and smooth the pesto. Pour a thin film of olive oil over the pesto to discourage discoloration. Cover the container and refrigerate until ready to use. (The pesto can be stored for up to 3 weeks, covered, and refrigerated. Bring to room temperature before using.)

Arugula Pesto: Substitute arugula leaves for the basil.

Note

Freezing Pesto: Pesto can be frozen in an airtight container (no need to film the pesto surface with oil) for up to 3 months. Grated cheese tends to get rubbery when frozen, so delete it when making the pesto. Add the cheese directly to the dish along with the pesto in the proportion of 2 tablespoons grated cheese for every 1/2 cup pesto. If you plan to use the pesto in small amounts, spoon the pesto into an ice cube tray and freeze until solid. Remove the pesto cubes from the tray and freeze them in a self-locking plastic freezer bag.

Basil

There are now almost countless varieties of basil at farmers' markets and nurseries, but the big-leafed, aromatic Genovese basil is probably the most familiar and the most useful. In the garden, it gets leggy and goes to seed fairly easily. To ensure a steady supply throughout the summer, plant some seedlings in the spring, and then another few plants in July, as the first batch is showing signs of flagging.

Store basil like a bouquet of flowers: trim the ends of the stems and stand the bunch in a glass of water. Tent a plastic bag over the top and refrigerate. Store-bought basil can be quite sandy, so wash it well before using. After cleaning, dry it in a salad spinner, then chop as needed.

Potato Salad with Green Beans and Pesto

Potato salad is a must at summer cookouts. Now, there is nothing wrong with the standard American potato salad with mayonnaise, but this pesto-tossed version works better when you have Mediterranean flavors on the menu. The color of the pesto may dull as it stands, so perk up the color with additional fresh herbs before serving. Serve this alongside the Grilled Chicken with Rosemary White Barbecue Sauce (page 61).

½ pound green beans, preferably flat Romano beans, trimmed and cut into 1-inch lengths

2½ pounds red potatoes, scrubbed

3 tablespoons Classic Basil Pesto (page 47)

2 tablespoons red wine vinegar

½ cup extra virgin olive oil

Salt and freshly ground black pepper

Chopped fresh basil or parsley

1. Bring a large pot of lightly salted water to a boil over high heat. Add the green beans and cook until tender, about 4 minutes. Using a skimmer or wire strainer, remove the green beans from the water and transfer to a bowl of cold water. Drain and pat dry with paper towels.

2. Add the potatoes to the water and return to a boil. Reduce the heat to medium and simmer the potatoes until they are tender when pierced with a sharp thin knife, about 25 minutes. Drain the potatoes in a colander and rinse under cold water until easy to handle. Slice the warm potatoes into ½-inch-thick rounds and transfer to a medium bowl.

3. Whisk the pesto, vinegar, and oil together. Pour over the potatoes, add the green beans, and mix. Season with salt and pepper to taste. Cover with plastic wrap pressed directly on the surface of the salad and cool. (The salad can be prepared, cooled, covered, and refrigerated up to 1 day ahead. Bring to room temperature before serving.) Sprinkle with the basil and serve at room temperature.

Grilled Corn and Bean Salad with Chile Vinaigrette

Makes 8 servings

With bright colors and vibrant flavors, this salad can really enliven a buffet. Make it a few hours ahead of serving so the ingredients have a chance to mingle. While grilling is my favorite way to cook corn, you could simply boil the corn before cutting off the kernels. If you and your guests like cilantro (I live in a cilantro-phobic household), add ⅓ cup chopped fresh cilantro to the salad just before serving.

3 ears corn

One 15- to 19-ounce can black beans, rinsed and drained

One 15- to 19-ounce can pinto or pink beans, rinsed and drained

4 ripe plum tomatoes, seeded and cut into ½-inch dice

1 medium sweet onion, such as Vidalia, Maui, or Walla Walla, finely chopped

CHILE VINAIGRETTE

Grated zest of 1 lime

3 tablespoons fresh lime juice

2 garlic cloves, crushed through a press

½ canned chipotle chile in adobo, with any clinging sauce, minced

¾ cup extra virgin olive oil

Salt and freshly ground black pepper

1 cup (4 ounces) crumbled queso fresco or ricotta salata

1. Build a hot fire in an outdoor grill. For a charcoal grill, let the coals burn until they are covered with white ash. For a gas grill, preheat the grill on high.

2. Strip the ears of their outer husks, leaving one final layer of husks attached. Grill the corn, turning occasionally, until the husks are charred, about 10 minutes. Cool until easy to handle. Discard the husks and silks. Cut the kernels from the corn. Mix the corn, black and pinto beans, tomatoes, and sweet onion in a large serving bowl.

3. To make the vinaigrette, combine the lime zest and juice, garlic, and chipotle in a blender. With the machine running, add the oil through the feed tube. Season with salt and pepper to taste. Pour over the salad and mix well. (The salad can be made, covered, and refrigerated up to 1 day ahead. Adjust the seasonings before serving.)

4. Just before serving, sprinkle with the cheese and serve chilled or at room temperature.

Corn

When it comes to corn, I don't care if it is white, yellow, or bicolor—I'll eat it. Hot from the pot or grill, cut off the cob and sautéed, it's all good. Some eaters are very particular about their preferences, but truly with new corn hybrids tempting the farmer, the consumer is at the mercy of what is marketed.

For example, white Silver Queen was long considered the ultimate in off-the-cob eating. Sweet but not sugary, with a crisp texture, it was the corn that I used to buy at farm stands up and down the eastern seaboard. Now it has been supplanted by easier-to-grow varieties. Personally, I don't even bother with out-of-season corn, which is so sweet that it makes my teeth hurt. (I exaggerate, but not much.)

Look for blemish-free ears of corn with fresh-looking, moist tassels. The corn should feel heavy for its size. Don't shuck the husks all the way back to check for blemishes and cutworms. First of all, this shortens the shelf life of the corn and, second, you can usually tell the quality of the ear by a quick peek at the tip. Cook the corn as soon after purchase as possible, as the starches in the corn convert to sugar as it stands. If you must, store the corn in the refrigerator. After reading an unsubstantiated report that salt toughens corn, I have stopped putting salt into the cooking water for boiling corn on the cob, but I could be overreacting.

Grilled Vegetable Salad with Tomato Vinaigrette

Makes 6 to 8 servings

With its colorful mix of purple eggplant, yellow summer squash, and red peppers on a bed of deep green arugula, this salad makes quite a bold appearance on the summer table. If you wish, top the salad with crumbled feta or ricotta salata. Leftovers are a welcome boon—just chop them up and toss with cooked ziti for a cool summer pasta salad.

2 medium white or graffiti eggplant, cut crosswise into $\frac{1}{2}$-inch-thick rounds (see Note)

2 large yellow squash, cut lengthwise into $\frac{1}{2}$-inch-thick strips

$\frac{1}{4}$ cup extra virgin olive oil, as needed, for brushing the vegetables

2 red bell peppers, prepared for grilling (see page 66)

2 ripe plum tomatoes, left whole

TOMATO VINAIGRETTE

2 ripe plum tomatoes, grilled (see above)

2 tablespoons red wine vinegar

1 garlic clove, crushed through a press

$\frac{1}{2}$ cup extra virgin olive oil

Salt and freshly ground black pepper

8 cups arugula leaves

2 scallions, white and green parts, chopped

1. Build a hot fire for direct cooking in an outdoor grill. For a charcoal grill, let the fire burn until the coals are covered with white ashes. For a gas grill, preheat on high.

2. Brush the eggplant and yellow squash all over with oil. The oil should be a very thin coating, as too much will drip onto the coals and cause flareups. Lightly oil the grill grate. Place the eggplant and yellow squash on the grill. Add the red peppers, skin side down, and the tomatoes to the grill. Grill and cut the vegetables as follows:

   Red bell peppers: Grill until the skin is charred and blistered, about 10 minutes. Let stand until cool, about 10 minutes. Remove the blackened skin. Cut into ½-inch-wide strips.
   Eggplant: Grill, turning occasionally, until the eggplant is tender, about 8 minutes.
   Squash: Grill until the undersides are seared with grill marks, about 3 minutes. Turn and cook until the squash is tender, about 3 minutes longer.
   Tomatoes: Grill until the undersides are seared with grill marks, about 2 minutes. Turn and cook until the skin is charred, about 4 minutes. Cut each tomato in half lengthwise and poke out and discard the seeds. Set the tomato halves aside for the vinaigrette.

   Let the red peppers, eggplant, and squash cool.

3. To make the vinaigrette, process the tomatoes, vinegar, and garlic in a blender. With the machine running, add the oil through the feed tube in the lid. Season with salt and pepper to taste. (The vegetables and vinaigrette can be prepared up to 8 hours ahead, covered, and stored at room temperature.)

4. Spread the arugula on a large serving platter. Arrange the red peppers, eggplant, and squash on top, and season lightly with salt and pepper to taste. Pour the tomato vinaigrette over the vegetables. Sprinkle with the scallions and serve.

Note   *Pale-skinned eggplants, such as the white or the striated light purple graffiti variety, are not as bitter as the traditional dark purple globe eggplant, and they do not need to be salted before cooking. If you only have globe eggplants, sprinkle the sliced rounds on both sides with salt and let stand in a colander in the sink for at least 1 hour to draw out excess bitter juices. Rinse the eggplants and pat dry with paper towels. The eggplants are now ready to grill.*

MAIN COURSES

Grilled Chicken with Rosemary White Barbecue Sauce

Spanish Burgers with Romesco and Manchego Cheese

Flank Steak with Manhattan Marinade

Grilled Pork Chops with Fresh Asian Plum Sauce

Grilled Hot Dogs with Quick Chowchow

Giant Zucchini with Lamb Stuffing

Soft-Shell Crab BLT Sandwiches

Lobster Rolls

Stockpot Clambake

Grilled Eggplant and Tomato Sandwiches

Corn Hotcakes with Blackberry Syrup

Grilled Chicken with Rosemary White Barbecue Sauce

Makes 6 to 8 servings

Many cooks in Alabama don't cotton to red barbecue sauce and finish grilled chicken with a mayonnaise-based slather. My version adds garlic and herbs to the formula, and the result is a great alternative to the typical backyard bird. Like all barbecue sauces, don't apply it to the chicken until the last few minutes. This one won't scorch like the sweet tomato sauces, but it could separate.

ROSEMARY WHITE BARBECUE SAUCE

1 1/3 cups mayonnaise

Grated zest of 1 lemon

1/2 cup fresh lemon juice

4 teaspoons chopped fresh rosemary

2 garlic cloves, crushed through a press

Two 4-pound chickens, each cut into 8 serving pieces

1 1/2 teaspoons salt

1/2 teaspoon freshly ground black pepper

1. To make the sauce, whisk the mayonnaise, lemon zest and juice, rosemary, and garlic together. (The sauce can be made up to 3 days ahead, covered, and refrigerated.)

2. Build a fire for indirect grilling in an outdoor grill. For a charcoal grill, leave the coals heaped in a mound in the center. For a gas grill, preheat on high. Then leave one burner on high and turn the other burner(s) off.

3. Season the chicken with the salt and pepper. Lightly oil the cooking grate. Place the chicken on the unheated areas of the grill (that is, on the perimeter around, but not over, the coals in the charcoal grill, or over the off burners of the gas grill). Cover and grill for 20 minutes. Turn the chicken, cover, and continue grilling until an instant-read thermometer inserted in the thickest part of the breast reads 165°F, about 20 minutes more.

4. Move the chicken to the hot area of the grill (over the coals of the charcoal grill, and over the high burner of the gas grill). Brush the chicken all over with the mayonnaise mixture. Grill, turning and basting occasionally with the remaining mayonnaise mixture, until the mayonnaise has reduced to a mostly transparent glaze, 3 to 5 minutes. Transfer to a platter and serve hot, with the remaining sauce passed on the side, if you wish.

Summer Holiday Cookout

Eggplant and Red Pepper Dip (page 21)

Assorted crackers and pita bread wedges

Grilled Chicken with Rosemary White Barbecue Sauce (page 61)

Potato Salad with Green Beans and Pesto (page 50)

Grilled Vegetable Salad with Tomato Vinaigrette (page 55)

Grilled Corn on the Cob with Jalapeño-Lime Butter (page 113)

Ice-cold beer

Berry Tiramisù (page 131)

Spanish Burgers with Romesco and Manchego Cheese

It's pretty difficult to go through summer without at least one cookout with sizzling burgers hot from the grill. There's nothing wrong with the all-American version and all the fixings, but I am very partial to these pared-down, Spanish-inspired burgers. Romesco, a roasted red pepper pesto, goes perfectly with the beef, and sharp Manchego cheese may just usurp Cheddar as the ultimate cheeseburger topping. Add sliced tomatoes and lettuce if you wish, but frankly, less is more here to appreciate the flavors better.

ROMESCO

1 large garlic clove, crushed under a knife and peeled

1/4 cup sliced natural almonds

2 red bell peppers, grilled, skins and seeds removed (see page 66)

2 teaspoons sherry vinegar or red wine vinegar

1 teaspoon sweet paprika, preferably smoked paprika, such as pimentón de la Vera

1/2 teaspoon dried oregano

3 tablespoons extra virgin olive oil

Salt and freshly ground black pepper

2 pounds ground round beef (85% lean)

2 teaspoons salt

1/2 teaspoon freshly ground black pepper

5 ounces Manchego cheese, thinly sliced

4 sourdough sandwich buns (pull out some of the inner crumb if the buns are too thick)

1. Build a fire for banked grilling in an outdoor grill. For a charcoal grill, let the coals burn until they are covered with white ash. Spread out the mound of coals into a bank, with one side about two coals deep, and the other side of the slope with a scattering of single coals. For a gas grill, preheat the grill on high. Leave one side on high and turn the other side to low. In both cases, you will have two areas for cooking, one hot and the other cooler.

2. To make the romesco, with the machine running, drop the garlic through the feed tube of a food processor fitted with the metal chopping blade to finely chop it. Add the almonds, red peppers, vinegar, paprika, and oregano. With the machine running, gradually add the oil, then season with salt and pepper to taste. Transfer the sauce to a bowl. (The romesco can be made up to 2 weeks ahead, covered, and refrigerated. Bring to room temperature before serving.)

3. Working as gently and quickly as possible (overmixing compacts the meat and makes tough burgers), mix the ground round, salt, and pepper. Lightly form into 4 patties about 4 inches wide. Make an indentation, about 2 inches wide and ½ inch deep, in the center of each burger to help it keep its shape during grilling.

4. Lightly oil the cooking grate. Place the burgers on the hot area of the grill. Cover and cook, turning once, until the outside is seared with grill marks, about 2 minutes per side. Move the hamburgers to the cooler side of the grill and cover. Cook, turning once, until the hamburgers feel somewhat firm but not resistant when pressed in the center, about 4 minutes for medium-rare. If using a meat thermometer, insert it horizontally through the side of the burger to reach the center; it should read 125°F. During the last 2 minutes, top each burger with the cheese, and place the buns on the grill to toast lightly and warm through.

5. Place a burger in each bun, top with a large dollop of romesco sauce, and serve immediately.

Sweet Bell Peppers

Red, yellow, purple, orange, chocolate brown, and as an afterthought, green . . . these are the main colors of sweet peppers that you are likely to come across at the farmers' market. You'll find a range of shapes too, from elongated Italian frying peppers to round cherry peppers. Allow the farmer to guide you in selecting an unfamiliar variety.

Buy firm peppers with no signs of shriveling or soft spots. In general, peppers change color as they ripen. A green pepper is simply an unripe pepper on its way to becoming another color, so it will be less sweet than a colored pepper. The ribs and seeds can be quite bitter, and must be removed before eating.

To prepare a bell pepper, cut off the top and bottom of the pepper to make "lids." Make a slit down the side of the pepper and open it up. Cut out and discard the ribs and seeds. The cored pepper can now be cut as needed.

To grill a pepper, place the cored pepper, skin side down, on a hot outdoor grill. Grill until the skin is blackened and blistered, about 8 minutes. Remove from the grill and cool until easy to handle. (Do not cover the pepper; covering creates steam that can soften the flesh.) Remove the blackened skin. The peppers can also be broiled, about 6 inches from the source of heat, to char the skin.

Flank Steak with Manhattan Marinade

Makes 4 servings

While Father's Day may not always officially occur during the summer, most people consider it a summer holiday and the perfect occasion for a backyard barbecue. And for many dads, a grilled steak is the celebratory dish of choice. When my dad and I are grilling together, we are often sipping Manhattan cocktails of bourbon and sweet vermouth (or Rob Roys, which substitute scotch for the bourbon). This marinade for flank steak uses our favorite drink as a springboard.

$\frac{1}{3}$ cup bourbon

$\frac{1}{3}$ cup soy sauce

3 tablespoons sweet vermouth

2 tablespoons light brown sugar

2 tablespoons peeled and finely chopped fresh ginger

1 scallion, white and green parts, chopped

2 garlic cloves, chopped

One 1 $\frac{1}{2}$-pound flank steak

1. Whisk the bourbon, soy sauce, sweet vermouth, brown sugar, ginger, scallion, and garlic together in a bowl to dissolve the sugar. Pour into a large self-locking plastic bag and add the steak. Close the bag and refrigerate for at least 4 and up to 8 hours. Remove from the refrigerator 1 hour before grilling.

2. Build a hot fire for direct grilling in an outdoor grill. For a charcoal grill, let the coals burn until they are covered with white ash. For a gas grill, preheat the grill on high.

3. Lightly oil the cooking grate. Remove the steak from the marinade. Place on the grill and cover the grill. Grill until the underside is well browned, about 3 minutes. Turn and grill until an instant-read thermometer inserted in the thickest part of the steak reads 130°F for medium-rare steak, about 3 minutes more. Transfer to a carving board and let stand 5 minutes.

4. Holding a sharp carving knife on a slight diagonal, thinly carve the steak across the grain. Serve hot, with the carving juices.

Grilled Pork Chops with Fresh Asian Plum Sauce

The secret to juicy grilled pork chops? Some folks like to brine them, but that is very problematic, as most markets sell pork that has already been injected with a saline solution. Simply grill thick-cut chops over medium, not searingly hot, heat, and you'll have moist, tender results. A savory-sweet fresh plum sauce rounds out the dish beautifully. As a side dish, offer a slaw made with napa cabbage and a rice vinegar dressing.

FRESH ASIAN PLUM SAUCE

2 teaspoons vegetable oil

2 scallions, white and green parts, chopped

2 tablespoons finely chopped fresh ginger

1 garlic clove, minced

1 pound fresh plums, pitted and cut into $\frac{1}{2}$-inch dice

$\frac{1}{4}$ cup packed light brown sugar

$\frac{1}{4}$ cup balsamic vinegar

2 tablespoons soy sauce

$\frac{1}{4}$ teaspoon five-spice powder

$\frac{1}{8}$ teaspoon crushed hot red pepper

1 teaspoon kosher salt

$\frac{1}{2}$ teaspoon garlic powder

$\frac{1}{2}$ teaspoon onion powder

$\frac{1}{2}$ teaspoon Chinese five-spice powder

$\frac{1}{4}$ teaspoon freshly ground black pepper

4 center-cut, bone-in pork chops, cut about 1 inch thick

1. To make the plum sauce, heat the oil in a heavy-bottomed medium saucepan over medium heat. Add the scallions, ginger, and garlic and cook, stirring often, until the garlic is fragrant, about 1 minute. Add the plums, brown sugar, vinegar, soy sauce, five-spice powder, and hot red pepper, and bring to a simmer, stirring often. Reduce the heat to medium-low and cook, stirring occasionally, until the plums are tender and the juices are thickened, about 15 minutes. Transfer to a bowl and cool completely.

2. Mix the salt, the garlic, onion, and five-spice powders, and the black pepper. Sprinkle all over the pork chops. Place on a plate, cover, and let stand at room temperature while building the fire.

3. Build a fire for banked grilling in an outdoor grill. For a charcoal grill, let the coals burn until they are covered with white ash. Spread out the mound of coals into a bank, with one side about two coals deep, and the other side of the slope with a scattering of single coals. For a gas grill, preheat the grill on high. Leave one side on high and turn the other side to low. In both cases, you will have two areas for cooking, one hot and the other cooler.

4. Lightly oil the cooking grate. Place the pork chops over the hotter area of the grill and cover the grill. Grill until the undersides are seared with grill marks, about 3 minutes. Turn, cover, and sear the other sides, about 3 minutes more. Move the chops to the cooler area of the grill. Grill, covered, until the pork chops feel firm when pressed in the centers with a finger, 12 to 15 minutes. Transfer to a platter and serve with the plum sauce.

Grilled Hot Dogs with Quick Chowchow

Makes 6 servings, 1 quart chowchow

There are a number of great Polish butchers around my town, so grilled hot dogs are often featured at our neighborhood cookouts. Great franks deserve great toppings, and this homemade relish fills the bill. Traditionally, quarts of bright yellow chowchow would be canned in the summer for use in the future, but modern cooks will probably prefer this "one-quart-at-a-time" method. To be sure that your franks are just hot and not incinerated, cook them over medium heat, not the hottest of hot.

CHOWCHOW

4 cups chopped green cabbage

½ sweet red bell pepper, seeds and ribs removed, cut into ½-inch dice

2 Kirby cucumbers, scrubbed, seeded, and cut into ½-inch dice

1 large onion, chopped

1 tablespoon kosher salt

1 cup distilled white vinegar

⅔ cup packed light brown sugar

1 teaspoon dry mustard

½ teaspoon celery seed

½ teaspoon crushed hot red pepper

¼ teaspoon ground turmeric

12 hot dogs, each pierced in a few places with a fork

12 hot dog buns

1. To make the chowchow, combine the cabbage, red bell pepper, cucumbers, onion, and salt in a large colander, and place the colander in the sink. Put a plate to fit inside the colander on top of the vegetables and weigh down with a few large, heavy cans of food. Let stand for 1 hour to drain off excess juices.

2. Bring the vinegar, brown sugar, mustard, celery seed, hot red pepper, and turmeric to a boil in a large nonreactive saucepan over high heat, stirring to dissolve the sugar. Add the vegetable mixture (do not rinse) and return to a boil. Reduce the heat to medium and simmer, uncovered, until the cabbage is crisp-tender, about 5 minutes.

3. Transfer the chowchow to a 1-quart canning jar or medium bowl and cool to room temperature. Cover and refrigerate overnight. (The chowchow can be made up to 3 weeks ahead, covered, and refrigerated.) Remove from the refrigerator 1 hour before serving.

4. Build a medium-hot fire for direct cooking in an outdoor grill. For a charcoal grill, let the coals burn down until you can hold your hand 1 to 2 inches over the coals for about 3 seconds. (This will take about 30 minutes for most brands of charcoal.) For a gas grill preheat on high, then reduce the heat to medium.

5. Lightly oil the cooking grate. Place the hot dogs on the grill and cover. Grill, turning the hot dogs occasionally, until they are heated through, about 8 minutes. During the last minute or so, place the hot dog buns on the grill to toast. Tuck the hot dogs in the buns and serve hot, with the chowchow passed on the side.

Giant Zucchini with Lamb Stuffing

Makes 4 to 6 servings

My neighbors are very generous with sharing their zucchini crop, especially the monster-sized ones. Scooped out into big boats, they are great for stuffing. Ground lamb may take some searching (look at halal, Israeli, or specialty butchers, although I can get it at my local natural foods supermarket), but if you can't find it, go with ground round beef. The fresh tomato sauce comes together quickly while the stuffed zucchini bakes. For a great side dish, serve with the Orzo with Toasted Corn and Scallions (page 117). Don't be daunted by the long ingredients list, as the steps are easy, and this dish is hard to beat for an end-of-summer family dinner.

STUFFED ZUCCHINI

1 very large zucchini, 12 to 14 inches long (about 1 pound, 12 ounces)

2/3 cup long-grain rice

2 tablespoons extra virgin olive oil

1 medium onion, chopped

2 garlic cloves, finely chopped

1 pound ground lamb

1/2 cup fresh bread crumbs

1 teaspoon dried oregano

1 teaspoon salt, plus more for salting the zucchini

1/2 teaspoon freshly ground black pepper

1 large egg, beaten

2 teaspoons tomato paste

TOMATO SAUCE

2 tablespoons extra virgin olive oil

¼ cup chopped shallot

1 garlic clove, minced

1¼ pounds ripe plum tomatoes, seeded and chopped

1 tablespoon chopped fresh dill

Plain yogurt, for serving

1. Position a rack in the center of the oven and preheat the oven to 375°F. Lightly oil a rimmed baking sheet.

2. To prepare the zucchini, cut it in half lengthwise. Using a dessertspoon, scoop out and discard the seeds and soft center area, leaving a ½-inch-thick shell. Sprinkle the cut surfaces lightly with salt and let stand while making the stuffing.

3. Meanwhile, bring a medium saucepan of lightly salted water to a boil over high heat. Add the rice and reduce the heat to medium. Cook, uncovered, at a brisk simmer until the rice is barely tender, about 15 minutes. Drain, rinse under cold water, and drain again. Set aside.

4. Heat the oil in a medium skillet over medium heat. Add the onion and garlic and cover. Cook, stirring occasionally, until the onion is tender, about 5 minutes. Transfer to a large bowl and cool slightly. Add the lamb, rice, bread crumbs, oregano, salt, and pepper. Make a well in the center, add the egg and tomato paste, and mix the egg and tomato paste together to combine. Use your clean hands to work the entire mixture together.

5. Pat the zucchini dry with paper towels. Place, cut sides up, on the baking sheet and fill with the stuffing. Bake, uncovered, until an instant-read thermometer inserted in the center of the stuffing reads 160°F, about 30 minutes.

6. While the zucchini is baking, make the tomato sauce. Heat the oil in a large skillet over medium heat. Add the shallot and garlic and cook, stirring occasionally, until the shallot is tender, about 3 minutes. Add the tomatoes and cover. Cook until the tomatoes give off their juices, about 5 minutes. Uncover and cook until the tomatoes are tender and the juices are reduced, about 10 minutes. Stir in the dill and season with salt and pepper. Keep warm.

7. Remove the zucchini from the oven and let stand for 5 minutes. Cut into large pieces and serve hot, topped with the tomato sauce and a dollop of yogurt.

Summer Squash

There's more to summer squash than zucchini. Look for golden zucchini, yellow pattypan squash, round Italian zucchini—they can all be cooked like their more familiar cousin.

Summer squash has a delicate taste that lends itself to matching with more assertive flavors. Herbs and garlic are two of the most common seasonings. Remember that the larger the squash, the less flavorful the flesh, so don't let that zucchini in the garden get out of hand and grow to the size of a Chihuahua.

Buy summer squash that looks crisp and firm, and pass over the ones with nicks or soft spots. Scrub them well under cold running water with a vegetable brush before cooking, as invisible grit can nestle in the skin.

Soft-Shell Crab BLT Sandwiches

Makes 4 sandwiches

There have been studies that prove that the crunchy sound of eating crisp food stimulates the appetite. Surely, along with the fresh, briny flavor, this is the attraction of the soft-shell crab, one of the true glories of summer eating. The best way to enjoy the crabs is to play up their crackly edible shell with a batter coating.

½ cup mayonnaise

2 teaspoons chopped fresh chives

1 teaspoon chopped fresh tarragon

6 slices thick-sliced bacon

2 large eggs

½ cup all-purpose flour

2 tablespoons cornstarch

¼ teaspoon salt

⅛ teaspoon freshly ground black pepper

4 soft-shell crabs, cleaned (see Note)

⅓ cup vegetable oil

4 soft sandwich buns, toasted

2 ripe tomatoes, cut into 8 thin slices

4 leaves green lettuce

1. Mix the mayonnaise, chives, and tarragon in a small bowl. Cover and refrigerate until ready to use.

2. Cook the bacon in a large skillet over medium heat until browned and crisp, about 8 minutes. Transfer to paper towels to drain. Cut each strip in half to make 12 pieces total. Pour out and reserve the bacon fat. Wipe the skillet clean with paper towels.

3. Line a baking sheet with wax paper. Whisk the eggs in a shallow dish. Mix the flour, cornstarch, salt, and pepper in a second dish. Dip each crab in the eggs, then in the flour to coat completely. Transfer to the baking sheet and refrigerate for 15 to 30 minutes to set the crust.

4. Heat the oil and reserved bacon fat in a large skillet over medium-high heat until the oil shimmers. Carefully add the crabs to the skillet. (The crabs could splatter, so be careful.) Cook until the undersides are golden brown, about 3 minutes. Using a thin slotted metal spatula, turn the crabs and cook to brown the other sides, about 3 minutes more. Using the spatula, transfer the crabs to paper towels to drain briefly.

5. Spread the buns with the herb mayonnaise. Top each bottom bun half with a crab, 3 bacon slices, 2 tomato slices, and a lettuce leaf, then the top bun half. Cut each sandwich in half and serve immediately.

Note

Soft-shell crabs are very perishable, and it is best to clean them at home. But not everyone cares to deal with live crabs, even if their claws are not sharp. If you have the fish vendor clean them for you, refrigerate them immediately (bring a cooler with you to the store), and cook the crabs within 8 hours after purchase. To clean the crabs yourself, use kitchen scissors to snip off the area on the front of the body that contains the eyes and mouth. Turn the crab over and lift up the flap covering the gills on one side of the crab. Snip away the gills, and repeat on the other side.

Lobster Rolls

In New England, the lobster roll is the quintessential summer sandwich. Except for the fact that lobster can be pricey outside of the areas where it is harvested, it is nothing fancy—just lobster salad stripped down to its essence of shelled meat, mayonnaise, and a few spices. Some fancy chefs add chopped celery or fennel, mustard, or fresh herbs, but most Yankees would disapprove. While the authentic roll is a rectangular, top-split white bread affair, hot dog buns work just fine. So when you see lobsters on sale, pounce, and dig into the taste of an Atlantic seaboard summer.

Two 1½-pound live lobsters

3 tablespoons mayonnaise

2 teaspoons fresh lemon juice

Celery salt

4 rectangular top-split sandwich rolls or hot dog buns

4 tablespoons (½ stick) unsalted butter, softened

1 cup shredded iceberg or Boston lettuce

1. Bring a very large pot of lightly salted water to a boil over high heat. Add the lobsters and cover. Return to a boil, then remove the lid. Boil until the lobsters are bright red, about 8 minutes. Drain and rinse under cold running water.

2. Remove the lobster meat from the shells. A heavy-duty shell cracker (which looks like a squat nutcracker) and poultry shears will help crack and cut through the shell. Remove all edible meat, red coral, and green tomalley from the shells, but discard the other viscera. Cut the lobster into ¾-inch chunks.

3. Mix the lobster meat with the mayonnaise and lemon juice, and season with the celery salt to taste. Stir in the coral and tomalley, if desired. Cover and refrigerate until chilled, at least 2 hours. (The lobster salad is best served the day it is made.)

4. Heat a large heavy skillet or griddle over medium-high heat. Spread the outsides of the rolls with the softened butter. Place the rolls in the skillet and cook, turning once, until golden brown, about 1 minute per side.

5. Fill each roll with an equal amount of lobster salad and lettuce and serve immediately.

Stockpot Clambake

A trip to the shore for a clambake complete with a wood fire and seaweed is not always in the cards. As an alternative, simmer the seafood and vegetables in a huge pot on the stove. This is a one-pot meal—as long as you have a huge pot. You'll also need some accoutrements like bowls to collect the shells and cobs, small bowls for the garlic butter, a few platters to hold the shellfish and sausage, serving bowls for the potatoes and corn, cups for the broth, nutcrackers to help remove the lobster shells, and perhaps thin seafood forks. It's all part of the fun.

BOUQUET GARNI

2 celery ribs with leaves, cut in half crosswise

6 sprigs fresh parsley

6 sprigs fresh thyme or ½ teaspoon dried thyme

¼ teaspoon whole black peppercorns

2 dried bay leaves

HERBED GARLIC BUTTER

½ pound (2 sticks) unsalted butter

3 garlic cloves, finely chopped

1 teaspoon dried basil

1 teaspoon dried oregano

6 dozen littleneck clams, well scrubbed

¼ cup yellow cornmeal, fine or stone-ground

Three 1½-pound live lobsters

12 medium red potatoes, scrubbed but unpeeled

6 small onions, peeled but left whole

1½ pounds kielbasa or other smoked sausage, cut into 6-inch lengths

6 ears corn, husked

Salt and freshly ground black pepper

2 lemons, cut into wedges

1. To make the bouquet garni, rinse a large piece of cheesecloth under cold water and squeeze it out. Wrap the celery, parsley, thyme, peppercorns, and bay leaves into a bundle in the cheesecloth and tie with kitchen string. Set aside.

2. To make the garlic butter, melt the butter and garlic in a medium saucepan over medium heat. Add the basil and oregano. Set aside.

3. Combine the clams and cornmeal in a large bowl and cover with cold water. Let stand for 30 minutes to 2 hours.

4. Fill a very large canning pot or stockpot half full of water and add the bouquet garni. Cover and bring to a full boil over high heat. One at a time, add the lobsters, head first, and cover tightly. Return to a boil and cook just until the shells turn bright red, about 8 minutes. Using tongs, transfer the lobsters to a large platter and set aside.

5. Add the potatoes and onions to the lobster cooking liquid in the pot. Leaving the bouquet garni in the pot, pour out the liquid, leaving just enough to cover the potatoes and onions. Cover tightly, bring to a boil, and cook for 10 minutes. Layer

the kielbasa and then the corn on top of the vegetables; do not add more water. Cover and cook until the potatoes are almost tender, about 10 minutes.

6. Drain and rinse the clams under cold running water. Place the clams on the corn, then arrange the lobsters on top of the clams. Cover tightly and cook until the clams open, about 10 minutes.

7. Using tongs and a wire skimmer, transfer the lobsters, clams, and sausage to a large platter, discarding any unopened clams, and transfer the corn, potatoes, and onions to bowls or platters. Season the vegetables with salt and pepper.

8. Reheat the garlic butter until hot and melted. Pour into 6 ramekins or custard cups. Taste the cooking broth, season with salt and pepper, and ladle into 6 soup cups. (Freeze leftover broth to use as a seafood stock in other recipes.) Serve immediately, with the garlic butter and lemons.

Grilled Eggplant and Tomato Sandwiches

Makes 4 sandwiches

Whether you make them for a warm-weather lunch or a relaxed supper with vegetable-loving friends, these sandwiches are sure to satisfy. Use a crusty bread with a close crumb; if the loaf is riddled with interior holes, the vegetables will fall out of the sandwiches.

1 large eggplant, cut crosswise into ½-inch-thick rounds

Kosher salt

Extra virgin olive oil, for brushing the eggplant

8 slices crusty rustic bread

4 tablespoons Classic Basil Pesto or Arugula Pesto (see page 47)

2 medium ripe tomatoes, sliced into ¼-inch-thick rounds

4 ounces rindless goat cheese (chèvre), crumbled

1. Toss the eggplant with 1½ teaspoons salt in a colander. Place in the sink and let stand for 1 hour to drain off excess juices. Rinse the eggplant under cold water and pat dry with paper towels.

2. Build a fire for banked grilling in an outdoor grill. For a charcoal grill, let the coals burn until they are covered with white ash. Spread out the mound of coals into a bank, with one side about two coals deep, and the other side of the slope with a scattering of single coals. For a gas grill, preheat the grill on high. Leave one side on high and turn the other side to low. In both cases, you will have two areas for cooking, one hot and the other cooler.

3. Lightly oil the cooking grate. Brush the eggplant on both sides with olive oil. Place over the hotter side of the grill and cover. Grill until the undersides are seared with grill marks, about 2 minutes. Turn and sear the other sides, about 2 minutes longer. Transfer to the cooler side of the grill, cover, and grill until the eggplant is tender, about 5 minutes. During the last minute or so, place the bread slices on the grill to toast them lightly.

4. Spread 4 bread slices with pesto. Place, pesto side up, on a work surface. Top each with equal amounts of the eggplant, tomatoes, and crumbled goat cheese. Top each with a slice of bread and cut in half crosswise. Serve immediately or cooled to room temperature.

A Summertime Picnic

Summer Minestrone, served in mugs (page 28)

Grilled Eggplant and Tomato Sandwiches (page 87)

Layered Salad with Creamy Sweet Onion Dressing (page 37)

Grilled Corn and Bean Salad with Chile Vinaigrette (page 52)

Blueberry Crumb Coffee Cake (page 134)

Corn Hotcakes
with Blackberry Syrup

Makes 12 pancakes, 4 to 6 servings

A long, relaxed weekend breakfast is the time to cook up a stack of hot pancakes. During the summer, why not take advantage of the time-honored combination of fresh corn and berries? When these hotcakes are served with a pile of browned sausage and lots of coffee, it's just possible that no one will want to get up from the table. Blueberries will also make fine syrup for your hotcakes.

BLACKBERRY SYRUP

1 pint blackberries

1½ cups maple syrup

CORN HOTCAKES

1 cup all-purpose flour

1 cup yellow cornmeal, preferably stone-ground

1 tablespoon sugar

1 teaspoon baking powder

½ teaspoon salt

1½ cups fresh corn kernels, cut from about 3 ears corn, divided

1½ cups whole milk

2 large eggs

Vegetable oil, for the griddle

Softened butter, for serving

1. To make the blackberry syrup, combine the berries and syrup in a medium saucepan. Bring to a boil over medium heat, stirring often. Reduce the heat to medium-low and simmer until the berries are tender and have given off their juices, about 5 minutes. Remove from the heat and keep warm.

2. To make the pancakes, preheat the oven to 200°F. Whisk together the flour, cornmeal, sugar, baking powder, and salt in a large bowl to combine. In a blender, process 1 cup of the corn kernels and the milk until the corn is pureed. Add the eggs and pulse to combine. Pour into the dry ingredients and stir just until smooth. Fold in the remaining ½ cup corn kernels.

3. Heat a griddle over high heat until the griddle is very hot. (A sprinkle of water will evaporate immediately.) Lightly oil the griddle. Using ¼ cup batter for each pancake, pour the batter onto the griddle. Cook until the tops of the pancakes are covered with bubbles, about 2 minutes. Turn the pancakes and cook until the undersides are golden brown, about 1 minute. Transfer to a baking sheet and keep warm in the oven until all of the pancakes are cooked.

4. Serve hot, with the syrup and butter passed on the side.

PASTA AND RISOTTO

Spaghetti with Shrimp and Arugula Pesto

Ratatouille Lasagna

Fettuccine with Creamy Zucchini Sauce

Spaghetti with Roasted Summer Vegetable Sauce

Ziti with Sausage, Sweet Peppers, and Corn

Risotto with Tomatoes, Basil, and Ricotta Salata

Spaghetti with Shrimp and Arugula Pesto

Sure, arugula is a fine salad ingredient, but it also makes a spicy and versatile pesto. Here it is mixed with shrimp and cherry tomatoes to dress spaghetti, a dish that will have you out of the kitchen in no time—something that is never more welcome than in the summer.

1 pound spaghetti

3 tablespoons extra virgin olive oil, divided

1 pound extra-large (21 to 26 count) shrimp, peeled and deveined

1 pint cherry tomatoes, cut in half lengthwise

Salt and freshly ground black pepper

½ cup Arugula Pesto (see page 48)

Freshly grated Parmesan, for serving

1. Bring a large pot of lightly salted water to a boil over high heat. Add the spaghetti and cook according to the package instructions just until tender. Scoop out and reserve ½ cup of the cooking liquid. Drain the spaghetti in a colander.

2. Meanwhile, heat 2 tablespoons of the oil in a large skillet over medium-high heat. Add the shrimp and cook, stirring occasionally, just until they turn opaque, about 2 minutes. Using a slotted spoon, transfer the shrimp to a plate.

3. Add the remaining 1 tablespoon oil to the skillet and heat. Add the cherry tomatoes and cook until they are heated through, about 2 minutes. Transfer to the plate with the shrimp. Season the shrimp and tomatoes with salt and pepper to taste.

4. Return the spaghetti to the warm pot. Add the shrimp and tomatoes with the pesto. Stir to combine, adding enough of the reserved cooking liquid to loosen the pesto. Season again with salt and pepper. Serve hot, with the Parmesan passed on the side.

Arugula

Like many cooks, I felt as if I had discovered a new world when I first read the cookbooks of British writer Elizabeth David. Her manner of writing was a kind of tough love: If you had a question about an ingredient, it was left to you to be intrepid enough to satisfy your curiosity.

One word challenged me time and again: *rocket*. There were no signs in the produce section for it and there weren't seed packets for it at the hardware store. Not until I went to France to study cooking did I first taste *roquette* and learn that the spicy-hot green was called "rocket" by the British.

When this esoteric green started showing up in the salads at restaurants I was frequenting in Berkeley and San Francisco, its name was again unfamiliar (and Italian): *arugula*. In the next few years, arugula became almost too popular and now you can get it at most grocery stores.

Arugula can be very sandy, so it needs to be thoroughly rinsed. After tearing off the tough stems, fill a sink with cold water and add the arugula. Let the leaves float in the water for a minute or two, so the grit can sink to the bottom. Taste a leaf or two and if you find grit, wash it again. Once the arugula is clean, whirl it dry in a salad spinner.

One thing is for sure—salad has become much more interesting ever since rocket became arugula.

Ratatouille Lasagna

You may not think of lasagna as a summer dish. But when you have a crowd to feed, if it is as light as this vegetarian version, lasagna can be a contender even in warm weather. Thanks to no-boil noodles and a rich sauce that doesn't take hours of simmering, it comes together much more quickly than the usual recipe. If your gang insists on meat in their lasagna, add 1 pound sweet Italian sausage, removed from its casing, sautéed until cooked through, and drained, to the finished sauce.

RATATOUILLE SAUCE

1 large zucchini, scrubbed and cut into $1/2$-inch dice

1 large eggplant, cut into $1/2$-inch dice

2 teaspoons kosher salt

$1/4$ cup extra virgin olive oil, divided

1 large onion, chopped

1 large red bell pepper, seeds and ribs removed, cut into $1/2$-inch dice

2 garlic cloves, finely chopped

One 28-ounce can chopped tomatoes in juice

One 8-ounce can tomato sauce

One 6-ounce can tomato paste

2 teaspoons dried oregano

$1/2$ teaspoon crushed hot red pepper

$1/2$ cup chopped fresh basil

Salt and freshly ground black pepper

One 15-ounce container ricotta

1 cup (4 ounces) freshly grated Parmesan

2 large eggs, beaten

$\frac{1}{4}$ teaspoon freshly grated nutmeg

$\frac{1}{4}$ teaspoon salt

$\frac{1}{8}$ teaspoon freshly ground black pepper

One 8-ounce package no-cook lasagna noodles

4 cups (1 pound) shredded mozzarella

$\frac{1}{4}$ cup (2 ounces) freshly grated Parmesan

1. To make the ratatouille sauce, toss the zucchini, eggplant, and kosher salt in a large colander and place in the sink. Let stand to drain off excess juices, about 1 hour. Rinse under cold running water, drain, and pat dry with paper towels.

2. Meanwhile, heat 2 tablespoons of the oil in a large saucepan over medium heat. Add the onion, red bell pepper, and garlic. Cook, stirring often, until the vegetables are tender, about 8 minutes. Transfer to a bowl.

3. Add the remaining 2 tablespoons oil to the saucepan and increase the heat to medium-high. Add the zucchini and eggplant and cook, stirring occasionally, until the vegetables soften, about 5 minutes. Return the onion mixture to the pot, and stir in the tomatoes with their juices, tomato sauce, tomato paste, oregano, and hot red pepper. Bring to a boil, stirring often. Reduce the heat to medium-low. Simmer, uncovered, until the eggplant is tender, about 20 minutes. Stir in the basil and season with salt and pepper.

4. To make the cheese filling, mix the ricotta and Parmesan, eggs, nutmeg, salt, and pepper.

5. Position a rack in the center of the oven and preheat the oven to 350°F. Lightly oil a 9 x 13-inch baking dish. Spread about 1 cup of the sauce in the pan. Top with 3 lasagna rectangles, side by side, but not touching. Spread with one-third of the ricotta mixture, 1 cup of the mozzarella, and 1 cup of the sauce. Top with 3 lasagna rectangles. Repeat the layering of the ricotta mixture, mozzarella, sauce, and lasagna rectangles two more times, ending with a layer of lasagna rectangles. Spread the remaining sauce completely over the lasagna noodles. Cover with aluminum foil. (The lasagna can be prepared up to 8 hours ahead, cooled, and refrigerated.)

6. Bake for 30 minutes. Remove the foil and sprinkle with the remaining 1 cup mozzarella and the Parmesan. Bake, uncovered, until the lasagna is bubbling throughout, about 20 minutes. Let stand for 10 minutes. Serve hot.

A Mediterranean-Style Supper

Arugula, Prosciutto, and Cantaloupe Salad (page 43)

Ratatouille Lasagna (page 98)

Crusty bread with extra virgin olive oil

Chilled Beaujolais

Plum Tart with Walnut Streusel Topping (page 154)

Fettuccine with Creamy Zucchini Sauce

Makes 4 to 6 servings

Here's another recipe for that time of summer when everyone with a garden is offering you summer squash. To give the zucchini a nice golden brown tinge and depth of flavor, do not salt the squash until after it has been sautéed. Otherwise, the salt will draw out the liquid and prevent proper browning. Since basil is as abundant as zucchini in the summer, it makes sense to use it in this recipe, but a substitution of 1 tablespoon finely chopped rosemary for the basil is nice, too.

¼ cup extra virgin olive oil, divided

2 large zucchini (or 1 zucchini and 1 yellow summer squash), scrubbed, cut lengthwise, and then cut into ¼-inch-thick half-moons

2 garlic cloves, finely chopped

Salt and freshly ground black pepper

1 pound fettuccine

1 cup ricotta

½ cup chopped fresh basil

Freshly grated Parmesan, for serving

1. Heat 2 tablespoons of the oil in a large skillet over medium-high heat. Add half of the zucchini and cook, stirring occasionally, until golden brown, about 6 minutes. Transfer to a bowl. Repeat with the remaining 2 tablespoons oil and zucchini. During the last minute of cooking the second batch of zucchini, stir in the garlic. Add to the bowl of zucchini. Season with salt and pepper to taste. Cover with aluminum foil to keep warm.

Pasta and Risotto

101

2. Meanwhile, bring a large pot of lightly salted water to a boil over high heat. Add the fettuccine and cook according to the package instructions just until tender. Scoop out and reserve ½ cup of the cooking water. Drain the pasta and return to the warm pot.

3. Add the zucchini and any juices and the ricotta to the pot. Mix, adding enough of the reserved cooking water to make a creamy sauce. Stir in the basil and season with salt and pepper.

4. Transfer to individual bowls and serve immediately, with a bowl of Parmesan passed at the table.

Spaghetti with Roasted Summer Vegetable Sauce

There's a dilemma to roasting vegetables in the summer. While the vegetables are at their peak, you may not want to heat up the kitchen from the oven. Just make this richly flavored sauce in the cool hours of the morning, and the problem is solved. You may want to make a double batch and store half for another meal.

SAUCE

Extra virgin olive oil

2 pounds ripe plum tomatoes, halved lengthwise and seeded

1 medium red bell pepper, seeds and ribs discarded, quartered lengthwise

1 medium yellow onion, peeled and quartered lengthwise

1 medium zucchini, scrubbed and cut into 1½-inch chunks

1 jalapeño chile, halved lengthwise, seeds and ribs discarded

Salt and freshly ground black pepper

1 large head garlic, unpeeled, cut in half crosswise

¼ cup chopped fresh basil

¼ cup chopped fresh oregano

1 pound spaghetti

Freshly grated Parmesan, for serving

1. To make the sauce, position an oven rack in the top third of the oven and preheat the oven to 450°F. Line a large rimmed baking sheet, such as a 12 x 17-inch "half sheet" pan, with aluminum foil, and oil the foil with some olive oil.

2. Arrange the tomatoes, red bell pepper, onion, zucchini, and jalapeño, cut sides up, on the pan. Brush with about 3 tablespoons olive oil. Season with salt and pepper to taste. Place the garlic, cut sides down, on the pan. Roast until the vegetables are tender and the edges are beginning to brown, about 30 minutes.

3. Cool until the vegetables are easy to handle. Remove the tomato skins and seeds from the tomato flesh and reserve both in a bowl. Strain the tomato skins and seeds in a wire sieve, pressing hard on them to remove the juices. Combine the tomatoes, strained juices, red pepper, onion, zucchini, and jalapeño in a food processor. Squeeze in the garlic flesh from the hulls. Add the basil and oregano. Pulse to make a coarsely chopped sauce. Season with salt and pepper. (The sauce can be made up to 2 days ahead, cooled, covered, and refrigerated.) Transfer to a saucepan. Cook over medium heat until simmering. Keep warm.

4. Meanwhile, bring a large pot of lightly salted water to a boil over high heat. Add the spaghetti and cook according to the package instructions. Drain well. Return the pasta to the warm cooking pot, add the sauce, and mix well.

5. Serve hot in individual bowls, with a bowl of Parmesan passed at the table.

Ziti with Sausage, Sweet Peppers, and Corn

One afternoon at the farm stand, it was impossible to choose among the array of perfect-looking vegetables, so I did what I often do: I bought a little bit of everything without any plan about how to cook it all. That evening, I made a dent in the mountain of produce with this deeply flavored pasta dish. Now I make it regularly, and shop accordingly.

3 tablespoons extra virgin olive oil, divided

3 plump links sweet Italian sausage (10 ounces), casings removed

1 medium red bell pepper, seeded and cored, cut into ½-inch dice

1½ cups fresh corn kernels (from 2 large ears corn)

2 scallions, white and green parts, chopped

2 garlic cloves, finely chopped

4 large ripe plum tomatoes, seeded and cut into ½-inch dice

¼ teaspoon crushed hot red pepper

¼ cup chopped fresh basil, plus more for garnish

Salt

1 pound ziti or other tubular pasta

½ cup freshly grated Parmesan, plus more for serving

1. Bring a large pot of lightly salted water to a boil over high heat. Begin the sauce while the water is heating.

2. Heat 1 tablespoon of the oil in a large skillet over medium heat. Add the sausage and cook, stirring occasionally and breaking up the sausage well with the side of a spoon, until the sausage is cooked through, about 8 minutes. Using a slotted spoon, transfer the sausage to a plate.

3. Add the remaining oil to the skillet and increase the heat to medium-high. Add the red bell pepper and corn and cook, stirring occasionally, until the pepper is tender, about 5 minutes. Stir in the scallions and garlic and cook until the garlic gives off its aroma, about 1 minute. Stir in the reserved sausage with the tomatoes and hot red pepper. Cook, stirring occasionally and scraping up the browned bits in the skillet, until the tomatoes give off their juices, about 5 minutes. Stir in the basil. Season with salt to taste.

4. Meanwhile, add the pasta to the water and cook according to the package instructions just until tender. Drain well. Return the pasta to the cooking pot. Stir in the vegetable mixture and the Parmesan. Correct the seasoning with salt.

5. Serve hot in individual bowls, topped with a sprinkle of basil, with Parmesan passed at the table.

Risotto with Tomatoes, Basil, and Ricotta Salata

Makes 4 main-course or 6 first-course servings

The first time I served this dish to friends, a collective sigh of appreciation rose from the table. I can't take too much credit, as the tomatoes were bursting with flavor and the basil was fresh from the garden, and that's a pretty good start for any recipe. While ricotta salata is becoming increasingly easy to find, if you can't get it, substitute Mexican queso fresco or even shredded mozzarella.

4 cups chicken broth, preferably homemade, or canned low-sodium broth

2 tablespoons extra virgin olive oil

1 medium onion, chopped

2 garlic cloves, finely chopped

2 cups risotto rice, such as Arborio, Carnaroli, or Vialone Nano

1 cup dry white wine, such as Pinot Grigio

2 large ripe beefsteak tomatoes, seeded and cut into ¾-inch dice

¼ cup chopped fresh basil

Salt and freshly ground black pepper

½ cup (2 ounces) ricotta salata

Freshly grated Parmesan, for serving

1. Bring the broth and 2 cups water to a boil in a medium saucepan over high heat. Reduce the heat to very low to keep the broth mixture hot.

2. Heat the oil in a heavy-bottomed large saucepan over medium heat. Add the onion and cook, stirring often, until softened, about 3 minutes. Add the garlic and cook until it gives off its aroma, about 1 minute.

3. Add the rice and cook, stirring often, until it turns from opaque to translucent and feels somewhat heavier in the spoon (do not brown), about 2 minutes. Add the wine and cook until almost evaporated, about 2 minutes.

4. About 1 cup at a time, stir the hot stock into the rice. Cook, stirring almost constantly, until the rice absorbs almost all of the stock, about 3 minutes. Stir in another cup of stock and stir until it is almost absorbed. Repeat, keeping the risotto at a steady simmer and adding more stock as it is absorbed, until you use all of the stock and the rice is barely tender, about 20 minutes total. If you run out of stock and the rice isn't quite tender, use hot water. When the risotto is almost done, stir in the tomatoes and basil. Season with salt and pepper to taste. Just before serving, stir in a final addition of broth; the risotto should have a loose, flowing consistency.

5. Spoon the risotto into individual bowls, and top each serving with the ricotta salata. Serve hot, with a bowl of Parmesan passed at the table.

SIDE DISHES

Grilled Corn on the Cob with Jalapeño-Lime Butter

Corn and Cheddar Pudding

Orzo with Toasted Corn and Scallions

Grilled Eggplant with Miso-Ginger Glaze

Peperonata

Zucchini and Radish Sauté

Grilled Corn on the Cob with Jalapeño-Lime Butter

Makes 6 servings

Grilled corn, cooked in its own package, gives even sweeter results than the traditional boiled method. Although it is often recommended, there's no need to soak the unhusked ears in water. Just pull back the husks to one final layer, and put the ears on the grill.

JALAPEÑO-LIME BUTTER

2 jalapeño chiles, roasted, peeled, and seeded (see page 7)

1 garlic clove, crushed through a press

Grated zest of 1 lime

½ cup (1 stick) unsalted butter, at room temperature

6 ears corn

Salt, for serving

---

1. To make the butter, process the jalapeños, garlic, and lime zest together in a mini food processor until finely minced. Add the butter and process until combined, scraping down the sides of the bowl as needed. (To use a blender, puree the jalapeños and garlic together in the blender. Transfer to a bowl, add the butter and zest, and mash with a rubber spatula until combined.) The butter can be prepared up to 8 hours ahead, covered, and stored at room temperature.

2. Build a hot fire for direct grilling in an outdoor grill. For a charcoal grill, let the coals burn until they are covered with white ash. For a gas grill, preheat on high.

3. Remove the corn husks, leaving the final husk layer and the corn silks attached. Place on the cooking grate (no need to oil the grate) and cover. Grill, turning occasionally, until the husks are seared all over with grill marks, about 10 minutes.

4. Wearing gloves or using kitchen towels to protect your hands, remove the corn husks and silk. Serve the corn immediately, with the butter and salt passed on the side.

Corn and Cheddar Pudding

Makes 6 servings

My mom's birthday is in July, and the family always throws a big backyard bash. While corn is at its peak and corn on the cob sounds like a great idea, we have learned that boiling up corn for a crowd is not so easy—especially cleaning up the eaten cobs. I have been serving this corn custard instead, and I always have to send out the recipe afterward.

For a large batch, double the recipe and bake in a 10 × 15-inch baking dish for about 40 minutes.

3 tablespoons unsalted butter (1 tablespoon softened), divided

½ red bell pepper, seeded and cored, cut into ¼-inch dice

2 scallions, white and green parts, finely chopped

1 garlic clove, chopped

2 cups fresh corn kernels (scrape the "milk" from the cobs, too), from 4 large ears, divided

¾ cup whole milk

3 large eggs

2 tablespoons yellow cornmeal

¾ teaspoon salt

¼ teaspoon freshly ground black pepper

1 cup (4 ounces) shredded extra-sharp Cheddar

2 tablespoons freshly grated Parmesan

1. Position a rack in the center of the oven and preheat to 325°F. Butter the inside of an 11½ x 8-inch baking pan with the 1 tablespoon softened butter.

2. Heat the remaining 2 tablespoons butter in a large skillet over medium-high heat. Add the red pepper and cook, stirring occasionally, until the pepper begins to soften, about 3 minutes. Stir in the scallions and garlic and cook until the scallions wilt, about 2 minutes. Transfer to a medium bowl and cool slightly.

3. Combine 1½ cups of the corn kernels and their "milk" with the whole milk in a blender. Process until the corn is pureed. Add the eggs, cornmeal, salt, and pepper, and pulse until combined. Stir into the vegetables. Add the Cheddar and the remaining ½ cup corn kernels and their "milk." Pour into the baking dish. Sprinkle with the Parmesan.

4. Bake until the top of the pudding is golden brown and feels set in the center, about 30 minutes. Remove from the oven and let stand for 5 minutes. (The pudding can be made up to 1 day ahead, cooled, covered, and refrigerated. Reheat, covered, in a microwave oven on medium until heated through, about 5 minutes. Do not overheat or the pudding could curdle.) Serve hot.

Orzo with Toasted Corn and Scallions

Makes 4 to 6 servings

As a side dish, this combination of rice-shaped pasta, toasted corn, and green scallions would go well with grilled meats, poultry, and fish. However, it is so tasty that it can also be a quick supper. In that case, add a big handful of cherry tomatoes to the corn to warm through during the last minute or so of cooking. The scallions act as the herb flavoring, but go ahead and replace them with a tablespoon or two of chopped fresh rosemary, dill, or basil if the spirit moves you.

1 cup orzo

1 tablespoon extra virgin olive oil

3 tablespoons unsalted butter, divided

1½ cups fresh corn kernels, cut from 2 large ears corn

2 small scallions, white and green parts, finely chopped

½ cup freshly grated Parmesan

Salt and freshly ground black pepper

1. Bring a medium saucepan of lightly salted water to a boil over high heat. Add the orzo and cook according to the package instructions until tender. Drain in a wire sieve, rinse under cold running water, and drain again. Toss the orzo with the oil and set aside.

2. Melt 2 tablespoons of the butter in a large nonstick skillet over medium-high heat. Add the corn and cook, stirring occasionally, until the corn is lightly toasted, about

5 minutes. Stir in the scallions and cook until the scallions are wilted, about 1 minute. Stir in the orzo with the remaining 1 tablespoon butter. Cook, stirring occasionally, until the orzo is hot, about 1 minute.

3. Transfer to a serving bowl. Stir in the Parmesan and season with salt and pepper to taste. Serve hot.

Grilled Eggplant with Miso-Ginger Glaze

Makes 6 servings

My farmers' market offers an embarrassment of eggplants—striped graffiti, lavender Japanese, and ivory white, in addition to dark purple eggplants of various shapes and sizes. This Asian-inspired recipe is best made with one of the small, elongated varieties. As a side dish, offer it with grilled teriyaki chicken or seared tuna steaks. It can also be served on a bowl of hot cooked rice as a vegetarian main course.

⅓ cup white miso

1 tablespoon dry sherry

1 tablespoon light brown sugar

1 teaspoon Asian sesame oil

2 tablespoons shredded ginger

6 small, elongated eggplants, such as graffiti or Japanese, 4 to 5 ounces each

Vegetable oil

1 scallion, white and green parts, finely chopped

---

1. Build a fire for banked grilling in an outdoor grill. For a charcoal grill, let the coals burn until they are covered with white ash. Spread out the mound of coals into a bank, with one side about two coals deep, and the other side of the slope with a scattering of single coals. For a gas grill, preheat the grill on high. Leave one side on high and turn the other side to low. In both cases, you will have two areas for cooking, one hot and the other cooler.

2. Mix the miso, sherry, brown sugar, and sesame oil in a small bowl. Stir in the ginger.

3. Cut the eggplants lengthwise. Using a thin sharp knife, lightly score the cut sides of the eggplants with a wide crosshatch pattern. Lightly brush the eggplants all over with vegetable oil. Place on the hotter area of the grill (that is, over the thick layer of coals in a charcoal grill, and on the high burner on a gas grill) and cover. Grill, turning once, until seared with grill marks on both sides, about 4 minutes. Move to the cooler part of the grill, cut sides up. Spread with the miso mixture. Cover and grill until the eggplant is very tender and the glaze is bubbling, about 10 minutes.

4. Transfer to a serving plate, sprinkle with the scallion, and serve hot.

Peperonata

One of the most colorful dishes to grace a table, peperonata is a useful blend of sautéed sweet peppers. Just some ideas: Serve it as a component of an antipasti spread, heap it on toasted bread as bruschetta, or top it with grilled salmon or swordfish. Start out with red and yellow peppers, and use whatever other colors your market offers. Keep in mind that chocolate or purple peppers lose their color when cooked, so don't be disappointed.

2 tablespoons extra virgin olive oil

4 sweet bell peppers, preferably 2 each red and yellow, seeded, cored, and cut into
½-inch-wide strips

1 large red onion, thinly sliced

2 garlic cloves, finely chopped

1 teaspoon dried oregano

¼ teaspoon crushed hot red pepper

3 tablespoons bottled capers, rinsed and drained

1 tablespoon red wine vinegar

1 teaspoon sugar

Salt

1. Heat the oil in a large skillet over medium heat. Add the bell peppers and onion and cover. Cook, stirring occasionally, until the vegetables begin to soften, about 3 minutes. Uncover and reduce the heat to medium-low. Cook, stirring occasionally, until the peppers are very tender but hold their shape, about 30 minutes.

2. Stir in the garlic, oregano, and hot red pepper and cook until the garlic gives off its aroma, about 1 minute. Stir in the capers, vinegar, and sugar and cook for 1 minute to blend the flavors. Season to taste with salt. Cool completely. (The peperonata can be prepared up to 1 week ahead, cooled, covered, and refrigerated.) Serve at room temperature.

Zucchini and Radish Sauté

Sautéed zucchini is a familiar side dish; sautéed radishes, not so. When cooked, radishes have a pleasant spiciness that perks up the zucchini. Fresh dill provides the final accent. If you have bright yellow zucchini, use it in tandem with the green variety for a very attractive dish.

2 tablespoons unsalted butter, divided

8 radishes, scrubbed and thinly sliced

2 medium zucchini, preferably 1 green and 1 golden, scrubbed and thinly sliced

1 tablespoon chopped fresh dill

Salt and freshly ground black pepper

1. Melt 1 tablespoon of the butter in a large skillet over medium-high heat. Add the radishes and cook, stirring often, just until they are beginning to heat through, about 1 minute.

2. Add the zucchini and cook, stirring often, until they are just tender, about 5 minutes. Stir in the dill and the remaining tablespoon of butter. Season with salt and pepper to taste. Serve hot.

DESSERTS

Mixed Berry Slump

Old-fashioned American fruit desserts can have odd names—grunt, cobbler, and betty, to name a few. A slump is berry compote simmered on the stove with dumplings on top. It's just the warm dessert to serve when you don't want to turn on the oven. Mix the berries to your liking, but don't overdo the strawberries, which lose much of their red color when cooked by themselves.

4 pints mixed berries, such as blueberries, blackberries, raspberries, and hulled, sliced strawberries

$^3/_4$ cup sugar, or more to taste

$^1/_2$ cup fresh orange juice

4 tablespoons unsalted butter

2 tablespoons cornstarch, dissolved in $^1/_4$ cup water

DUMPLINGS

2 cups all-purpose flour

3 tablespoons sugar

2 teaspoons baking powder

$^1/_4$ teaspoon salt

8 tablespoons (1 stick) unsalted butter, chilled and thinly sliced

$^2/_3$ cup whole milk

$^1/_2$ teaspoon vanilla extract

Vanilla ice cream

1. Combine the berries, sugar, orange juice, and butter in a nonreactive, heavy-bottomed saucepan or Dutch oven. Bring to a boil over medium heat, stirring to dissolve the sugar. Cook until the berries give off their juices, about 5 minutes. Stir in the dissolved cornstarch and return to the boil. Reduce the heat to medium-low.

2. Meanwhile, make the dumplings. Whisk the flour, sugar, baking powder, and salt in a bowl. Add the butter, and using a pastry blender or a large fork, cut the butter into the flour mixture until the mixture looks crumbly with a few pea-sized pieces of butter. Mix the milk and vanilla in a measuring cup and stir into the flour mixture.

3. Drop the dough by heaping teaspoons into the simmering berries to make 16 dumplings. Cover the saucepan and simmer until the dumplings are cooked through, about 20 minutes. Remove the pan from the heat and let stand, with the lid ajar, to cool slightly, about 10 minutes.

4. Serve the berries warm in individual bowls, each serving topped with 2 dumplings and a scoop of ice cream.

Berry Tiramisù

Red currants are another summer fruit that make a fleeting, but welcome, appearance in my farmers' market. They work best in tandem with other fruits, where their tangy juices can mingle with sweet flavors. This tiramisù is one of my favorite ways to show off the berries of the season. And if you're looking for a red, white, and blue dessert for Independence Day, this is it! (If currants haven't come into season in your area by then, substitute more raspberries for the currants.)

---

1 pint red currants, pulled off their stems with the tines of a fork

1 1/2 pints blueberries, divided

3/4 cup granulated sugar

1 pint raspberries, divided

12 Italian-style ladyfingers (*savoiardi*)

One 16- to 17.5-ounce container mascarpone, at room temperature

1/3 cup confectioners' sugar

1/3 cup heavy cream

---

1. At least 8 hours before serving the tiramisù, combine the currants, 1 pint of the blueberries, and the granulated sugar in a heavy-bottomed medium saucepan. Bring to a boil over medium heat, stirring occasionally to dissolve the sugar. Reduce the heat to medium and simmer, uncovered, until the berries give off their juices, about 5 minutes. Add 1/2 pint of the raspberries and cook until they are heated through but still hold their shape, about 2 minutes. Remove the berry sauce from the heat and cool.

2. Spoon half of the berry sauce into an 11 1/2 x 8-inch baking dish. Arrange the ladyfingers in the dish, trimming them as necessary to fit the dish. Top with the remaining berry sauce. Let stand 10 minutes so the ladyfingers can absorb the berry sauce.

3. Using a rubber spatula, mash the mascarpone, confectioners' sugar, and heavy cream in a medium bowl until combined. Do not overmix or the mascarpone could separate. With two applications, spread the mascarpone mixture over the ladyfingers. Top with the remaining blueberries and raspberries. Cover loosely with plastic wrap and refrigerate until chilled, at least 4 hours. (The tiramisù can be made and refrigerated up to 1 day ahead.) Serve chilled.

Red Currants

Don't confuse tart, red fresh currants with the raisinlike dried currants. The latter are actually dried fruits made from small grapes named after Corinth (*Coruntz* in Old French). You may find black currants at some farmers' markets, but they are so sour that they really need to be sweetened with loads of sugar and turned into a jam or preserve.

Blueberry Crumb Coffee Cake

I spent many summers in the Berkshire Mountains with friends who had blueberry bushes on their property. While we had to fight the birds for the berries, we still had so many that I had to become proficient in blueberry baked goods. This crumb cake made many appearances as a breakfast coffee cake or afternoon treat. Like all good crumb cakes, the balance of crumb to cake is almost equal. For easy removal of the cake from the pan, bake it in a springform pan.

CAKE

Butter and flour, for the pan

2 cups all-purpose flour

2 teaspoons baking powder

½ teaspoon salt

4 tablespoons (½ stick) unsalted butter, at room temperature

¾ cup granulated sugar

1 large egg, at room temperature

½ cup whole milk

1 pint fresh or frozen blueberries

TOPPING

1½ cups all-purpose flour

12 tablespoons (1½ sticks) unsalted butter, at room temperature

1 cup granulated sugar

½ teaspoon ground cinnamon

Confectioners' sugar, for serving

1. Position a rack in the center of the oven and preheat the oven to 350°F. Butter a 9-inch springform pan, dust with flour, and tap out the excess flour.

2. To make the cake, sift the flour, baking powder, and salt together. Beat the butter and sugar in a medium bowl with an electric mixer on high speed until the mixture is pale and gritty, about 2 minutes. Beat in the egg. Starting with the flour, alternate three equal additions of the flour with two equal additions of the milk, beating after each addition until the batter is smooth, and scraping down the sides of the bowl with a rubber spatula. Fold in the blueberries. Spread in the pan.

3. To make the topping, use your fingers to work the flour, butter, granulated sugar, and cinnamon into large crumbs. Scatter the crumbs evenly over the batter.

4. Bake until a wooden toothpick inserted in the center of the cake comes out clean, about 1 hour. Cool on a wire cake rack for 10 minutes. Remove the sides of the pan, then cool completely. (The cake can be stored at room temperature, wrapped in plastic wrap, for up to 3 days.)

5. Sift confectioners' sugar over the cake. Using a serrated knife, cut into wedges and serve.

Melt-in-Your-Mouth Blueberry Muffins

Feeding a summer home full of family and houseguests can keep a cook pretty busy. It's especially nice to serve freshly made baked goods warm from the oven. Is there a better way to start the day than to the aroma of hot muffins? Blueberry muffins are always popular, and sour cream gives these a very tender, cakelike crumb.

2 cups all-purpose flour

$\frac{2}{3}$ cup sugar

$\frac{1}{2}$ teaspoon baking soda

$\frac{1}{2}$ teaspoon baking powder

$\frac{1}{4}$ teaspoon salt

2 large eggs

1 cup full-fat sour cream

5 tablespoons ($\frac{1}{2}$ stick plus 1 tablespoon) unsalted butter, melted and cooled slightly

$1\frac{1}{2}$ cups fresh or frozen blueberries

1. Position a rack in the center of the oven and preheat the oven to 350°F. Line 10 muffin tins with paper liners.

2. Sift the flour, sugar, baking soda, baking powder, and salt together into a medium bowl. Beat the eggs until combined in another medium bowl, then stir in the sour cream and melted butter. Add to the dry ingredients and stir just until moistened. Fold in the blueberries. Spoon equal amounts of the batter into each muffin tin.

3. Bake until the muffin tops are golden brown and a wooden toothpick inserted in the center of a muffin comes out clean, 20 to 25 minutes. Cool in the tins for 5 minutes, then transfer to a wire cake rack. Serve warm or cooled to room temperature. (The muffins are best served the same day that they are baked. Freeze leftovers, stored in self-locking plastic bags, for up to 2 months. Defrost at room temperature.)

Cantaloupe Ice Pops

How many of us have memories of cooling off by eating ice pops on a hot summer afternoon? Of course, homemade pops made with fresh fruit are healthier than anything that I ever ate while sitting on our front porch. For the most flavorful pops, make these treats with the sweetest, ripest melon that is perhaps just a day away from having to be discarded.

½ ripe cantaloupe, peeled, seeds removed, cut into chunks

½ cup sugar

Grated zest of 1 lime

1½ tablespoons fresh lime juice

1. Puree the cantaloupe in a blender and measure: you should have 2 cups. Return the puree to the blender and process with ¾ cup water, the sugar, and the lime zest and juice. Pour equal amounts into 8 ice-pop molds. Cover each mold with its lid and insert a wooden stick.

2. Freeze until the pops are solid, at least 4 hours or overnight. Remove the pops from the molds and serve.

Chocolate Cherry Parfaits

These indulgences are a variation on cherries jubilee, but fresh cherries have it all over the typical canned fruit version. While the parfaits look innocent, the sauce does have a mild kick from the kirsch, so when serving to kids, substitute water for the kirsch. Splurge on a good bottle of kirsch, which will last forever. Kirsch is always expensive due to the amount of cherries used to create the heady eau-de-vie.

CHOCOLATE SAUCE

½ cup heavy cream

3 ounces bittersweet chocolate, finely chopped

2 tablespoons light corn syrup

CHERRY SAUCE

1½ cups pitted Bing cherries

6 tablespoons sugar

1½ teaspoons cornstarch

1½ tablespoons kirsch, cherry brandy, or brandy

1 pint vanilla ice cream

Sweetened whipped cream, for serving

4 fresh cherries with their stems, for garnish

1. To make the chocolate sauce, heat the cream in a small saucepan over medium heat. Remove the saucepan from the heat and add the chocolate. Let stand a few minutes until the chocolate softens, then whisk until smooth. Whisk in the corn syrup. Transfer to a bowl to cool completely.

2. To make the cherry sauce, cook the cherries and sugar in a saucepan over medium heat, stirring often, until the sugar is dissolved and the cherries give off their juice, about 5 minutes. Sprinkle the cornstarch over the kirsch in a small bowl and stir to dissolve the cornstarch. Stir into the cherries and cook just until the juices thicken. Transfer to another bowl and cool completely. (The chocolate and cherry sauces can be prepared up to 2 days ahead, cooled, covered, and refrigerated. Gently reheat the chocolate sauce just until fluid.)

3. Scoop equal amounts of the ice cream into 4 parfait or martini glasses, adding the chocolate and cherry sauces to get a layered effect. Top each with a dollop of whipped cream and a fresh cherry. Serve immediately.

Donut Peaches in Rosemary Syrup with Blackberries

Makes 6 servings

Donut peaches are one of the sweetest varieties, but because the white flesh clings stubbornly to the pit, they aren't my first choice for baked goods. However, simmered whole in beautifully aromatic rosemary syrup, and given a balancing touch of acidity from blackberries, these peaches offer up one of the most elegant desserts you can serve. Do serve it with a knife so your guests can cut the fruit away from that obstinate pit, a spoon to savor the syrup, and perhaps some cookies to round it all off.

2 cups dry white wine, such as Pinot Grigio

½ cup sugar

Six 2-inch-long rosemary sprigs

6 firm-ripe donut peaches, peeled (see page 153)

1 pint blackberries

1. Bring the wine, sugar, and rosemary to a boil in a large, deep skillet over high heat, stirring to dissolve the sugar. Add the peaches and reduce the heat to medium-low. Cover and simmer, turning the peaches over after 5 minutes, until the peaches are just tender when pierced with a sharp knife, about 10 minutes.

2. Using a slotted spoon, transfer the peaches to a 9 x 13-inch dish. Pour the syrup over the peaches. Let cool until tepid. Cover with plastic wrap and refrigerate until chilled, at least 4 hours or overnight. (The peaches can be refrigerated for up to 1 day ahead.)

3. To serve, transfer each peach to a bowl. Add equal amounts of berries to the bowls, and divide the syrup among the bowls. Serve chilled, with a spoon and a knife to cut the peach flesh away from the pit.

Gooseberry-Ginger Fool

I saw cartons of fresh gooseberries at the farmers' market, and had to experiment. They are most often used to create one of the classic British desserts, gooseberry fool. This is really no more than whipped cream and gooseberry sauce (I add crumbled cookies for some crunch), but it's quite delicious in its own humble way.

1 ½ pints gooseberries, husked, stems and tough tips removed, plus 4 gooseberries with
　　husks pulled back to reveal the berries, for garnish
½ cup granulated sugar, or more to taste
1 cup heavy cream, chilled
3 tablespoons confectioners' sugar
1 cup coarsely crumbled gingersnap cookies

1. Combine the gooseberries, granulated sugar, and 2 tablespoons water in a heavy-bottomed saucepan. Bring to a boil over medium heat, stirring to dissolve the sugar. Reduce the heat to medium-low and simmer until the gooseberries give off their juices, about 10 minutes. Strain the gooseberries in a wire sieve over a bowl, reserving the juices. Transfer the drained gooseberries to another bowl and set aside.

2. Return the juices to the saucepan and boil over high heat until syrupy, about 5 minutes. Taste the syrup, and if too tart, stir in more sugar until dissolved. Using a fork, crush the gooseberries in the bowl, and stir in the syrup. Refrigerate the syrup until chilled, at least 1 hour or overnight. (The sauce can be made, covered, and refrigerated up to 3 days ahead.)

3. In a chilled bowl, whip the cream and confectioners' sugar with an electric mixer on high speed until soft peaks form. Fold in the cookies. (The whipped cream can be made, covered, and refrigerated up to 8 hours ahead.)

4. Spoon a couple of tablespoons of the gooseberry sauce into each of 4 martini glasses or small bowls. Divide the whipped cream mixture among the glasses, then top each with equal amounts of the remaining sauce. Garnish each with a whole gooseberry. Serve chilled.

Gooseberries

Tasted raw, gooseberries are not the most delicious fruit. Sour is the first word that comes to mind, their flavor and papery husk indicating a close relation to the tomatillo. But when they are sweetened and cooked into a sauce, they show their stuff.

Gooseberries take a bit of prep work. Peel off the husk, and "top and tail" the stem and blossom end from each berry. Save a few unhusked berries to use as a dramatic garnish. Peel back the husk from each berry, keeping it attached at the stem end, to create a "petal" look.

Nectarine Clafoutis

Most American bakers aren't familiar with clafoutis, the classic French dessert. It has the creamy texture of custard, yet it can be cut like a cake. Besides being impossibly luscious, it is also easy to make. Try to serve it warm from the oven, or heat it very briefly in the microwave, just enough to take the chill off.

3 tablespoons unsalted butter, melted, divided

½ cup plus 2 tablespoons granulated sugar, divided

1½ cups whole milk

4 large eggs, at room temperature

2 tablespoons Cognac, brandy, or peach schnapps

1 teaspoon vanilla extract

1¼ cups all-purpose flour

¼ teaspoon salt

3 ripe nectarines, pitted and cut into ½-inch-thick wedges

¼ cup finely chopped crystallized ginger

Confectioners' sugar, for serving

1. Position the rack in the center of the oven and preheat the oven to 375°F. Brush the inside of a 9 x 2-inch round cake pan with some of the melted butter, reserving the remaining butter. Sprinkle 2 tablespoons of the sugar on the inside of the pan, tilt the pan to coat, and tap out the excess sugar.

2. Whisk the milk, eggs, remaining ½ cup sugar, reserved butter, Cognac, and vanilla in a bowl until well combined. Add the flour and salt and whisk until combined.

3. Arrange the nectarines in overlapping circles in the pan and sprinkle with the ginger. Gently pour in the batter. Bake until the clafoutis looks set in the center, about 40 minutes. Transfer to a wire cake rack and cool until warm, about 30 minutes.

4. Sift confectioners' sugar over the top, cut into wedges, and serve warm or cooled to room temperature. (The clafoutis can be stored in the refrigerator for up to 2 days.)

Sour Cream Peach Pie

Everyone knows the saying "as easy as pie." For many cooks, that's an oxymoron, as piecrust just isn't that easy to make. But this pie, with its simple cream cheese crust and seductive sour cream filling, laden with juicy peaches, can be mastered by a novice. And what results! The pie is best completely cooled or even chilled, so be sure to allow the extra time.

Cream Cheese Pie Dough for one 9-inch pie (see page 158)

FILLING

1 cup full-fat sour cream

¾ cup granulated sugar

1 large egg

2 tablespoons all-purpose flour

1 teaspoon vanilla extract

¼ teaspoon almond extract

¼ teaspoon salt

3 cups peeled, pitted, and sliced peaches (from 5 ripe peaches)

TOPPING

½ cup all-purpose flour

⅓ cup light brown sugar

4 tablespoons (½ stick) unsalted butter, at room temperature

¼ teaspoon ground cinnamon

1. Position a rack in the lower third of the oven and preheat to 400°F.

2. Place the dough on a lightly floured work surface, and sprinkle lightly with flour. Roll out the dough into a 13-inch round about ⅛ inch thick. Fit into a 9-inch pie dish. Fold the dough over so the edge is flush with the edge of the pan and flute the dough. Place the dough-lined pie pan in the freezer for 15 minutes.

3. To make the filling, whisk the sour cream, granulated sugar, egg, flour, vanilla and almond extracts, and salt together in a medium bowl. Fold in the peaches. Pour into the piecrust. Place on a rimmed baking sheet. Bake until the filling is almost completely set and beginning to brown around the edges, about 30 minutes.

4. Meanwhile, make the topping. Using your fingers, work the flour, brown sugar, butter, and cinnamon together in a small bowl until crumbly. When the pie filling is almost set, remove the pie on the baking sheet from the oven, and sprinkle the topping evenly over the filling. Return to the oven and reduce the temperature to 350°F. Bake until the filling is puffed and the topping is golden brown, 20 to 30 minutes longer. Transfer the pie to a wire cake rack and cool completely. (The pie is best the day it is made. Leftovers, covered and refrigerated, can be stored for up to 2 days.)

Peaches and Nectarines

It's difficult to pick a single favorite summer fruit, but peaches are certainly at the top of my list. Assuming that your peaches are perfectly ripened and filled with sweet juices, there are other characteristics that identify these fruits. Does the fruit fall cleanly away from the stone, or does it cling to the pit? (Fruits like peaches, plums, and apricots are called "stone fruits" for their rock-hard pits.) Is the fruit golden or pale?

As the summer progresses, so do the peach varieties. In late spring, cling peaches are the first to arrive. Next come the squat donut peaches and their cousins, white peaches. And finally, the large freestone peaches, with their fully developed flavor and bright gold interiors. Somewhere in there, smooth-skinned nectarines also show up. In general, white-fleshed peaches are less acidic than the yellow varieties. The sweetness of the former may make them best for eating out of hand, and the latter are usually preferred for pies and other baked goods.

When you are choosing peaches, don't just rely on touch to determine ripeness. Squeezing the fruit bruises it, and nine times out of ten, the fruit will feel hard anyway, so you are wasting your time. If the fruit is tinged with green, it has been picked too early and may take extra time to ripen. If you pick up the fruit, do so to smell it—the best peaches will give off a fruity perfume. Let the peaches ripen at room temperature. If you need to hurry ripening, close them in a paper (not plastic) bag.

Peach skin isn't that tasty and should be removed when making a filling for baked goods. To peel peaches, drop the fruit into a pot of boiling water. Blanch for about 30 seconds, or until the skin feels loosened (lift out the fruit with a slotted spoon to check). Transfer to a large bowl of ice water and let stand until easy to handle. Remove the skin with a small sharp knife. Stubborn skins can also be removed with a vegetable peeler.

Plum Tart with Walnut Streusel Topping

Turn to this formula (press-in dough, fresh fruit sprinkled with sugar and butter, topped with streusel) to make an easy but impressively professional-looking tart with almost any summer stone fruit. Peaches, apricots, pluots, and nectarines all take well to the tart treatment, but plums really shine. Do not add any thickener to the fresh fruit, as the juices will thicken and evaporate into a glaze during baking.

TART DOUGH

1 cup all-purpose flour

3 tablespoons granulated sugar

¼ teaspoon salt

6 tablespoons (¾ stick) unsalted butter, cut into tablespoons and chilled

1 large egg yolk

7 ripe red or black plums, pitted and cut into eighths lengthwise

3 tablespoons granulated sugar

½ cup all-purpose flour

⅓ cup light brown sugar

4 tablespoons (½ stick) unsalted butter, at room temperature

¼ teaspoon ground cinnamon

½ cup finely chopped walnuts

1. Position an oven rack in the bottom third of the oven and preheat the oven to 400°F.

2. To make the dough, pulse the flour, granulated sugar, and salt in a food processor fitted with the metal chopping blade to combine. Add the butter and pulse about 8 times until the mixture resembles coarse cornmeal with some pea-sized pieces. Add the egg yolk and pulse a few more times until the dough is moistened and crumbly. If you press the crumbs together between your fingers, it should hold together. Do not process until the dough forms a ball. Transfer the crumbly dough to a bowl and knead lightly until it comes together.

3. Crumble the dough into a 9-inch tart pan with a removable bottom. Press the dough firmly and evenly into the bottom, and then up the sides, of the pan. Take care that the dough isn't too thick in the corners where the sides and bottom meet, but forms a neat 90-degree angle as much as possible. Arrange the plums in concentric circles in the tart shell. Sprinkle with the granulated sugar.

4. Mix the flour, brown sugar, butter, and cinnamon in a small bowl with a rubber spatula until combined. Add the walnuts and work them in with your fingers. Crumble the walnut topping over the plums.

5. Place the tart pan on a rimmed baking sheet. Bake for 10 minutes. Reduce the heat to 350°F and bake until the plum juices are bubbling and the crust is golden brown, about 40 minutes. Transfer to a wire cake rack and cool. (The tart can be covered and stored at room temperature for up to 2 days.)

6. Remove the sides of the pan, cut into slices, and serve.

Raspberry and Almond Scones

My friend Michelle Grevesen shared her grandmother's recipe for scones, which we gussied up one morning with fresh raspberries and cubes of almond paste to make them even more special. If you want scones for breakfast, and want to save time, prepare and refrigerate the different components (flour/butter, liquids, and mix-ins) the night before and just mix them together in the morning.

1¾ cups all-purpose flour, plus more for the baking sheet

1 tablespoon sugar

2¼ teaspoons baking powder

¼ plus ⅛ teaspoon salt, divided

4 tablespoons (½ stick) unsalted butter, chilled, cut into tablespoons

2 large eggs

⅓ cup heavy cream

½ teaspoon almond extract

½ pint fresh raspberries

2 ounces almond paste or marzipan, cut into ¼-inch dice

2 tablespoons sliced almonds

1. Position a rack in the top third of the oven and preheat the oven to 400°F. Line a baking sheet with parchment paper or a silicone baking pad, and lightly dust with flour.

2. Sift the flour, sugar, baking powder, and ¼ teaspoon salt together into a medium bowl. Add the butter. Using a pastry blender, cut the butter into the flour mixture until the

butter pieces are about ¼ inch square. The mixture should have a rough texture, just short of the coarse-crumbs consistency used to make pastry dough.

3. Beat the eggs and the remaining ⅛ teaspoon salt in a small bowl until the eggs are well combined. Transfer 2 tablespoons of the beaten egg to another small bowl and set aside. Add the heavy cream and the almond extract to the remaining, larger portion of eggs and mix to combine. Pour into the dry ingredients and stir just until moistened. Add the raspberries and almond paste and stir just until the dough holds together.

4. Gather up the dough and place on the lined baking sheet. Using floured hands, pat the dough into a ¾-inch-thick round. Using a sharp knife, cut into 6 equal wedges, but do not separate them. Brush the scones with some of the reserved beaten egg, then sprinkle with the almonds.

5. Bake until the scones are golden brown, about 20 minutes. Serve warm or cooled to room temperature. (The scones are best served the day they are baked.)

Cream Cheese Pie Dough

Makes enough for two 9-inch piecrusts

For me and other people who love to bake, summer is a progression of one home-baked fresh-fruit pie after another. I'll start with early apricots and move on to sour cherries, then to peaches and blueberries. And I can do it because I have a good, easy pie dough recipe. Admittedly, traditional dough made with shortening or butter requires skill (if not old-fashioned guesswork) when it comes to adding the water to the dough. This dough is moistened with cream cheese, which contains just the right amount of liquid, eliminating the guesswork. The cheese's dairy fat contributes to the baked crust's melting tenderness, flaky crumb, and rich flavor.

1⅓ cups all-purpose flour

¼ teaspoon salt

10 tablespoons (1¼ sticks) unsalted butter, chilled, cut into tablespoons

6 ounces cream cheese (not low fat), at room temperature, cut into ¾-inch pieces

1. Put the flour and salt in a food processor fitted with the metal chopping blade and pulse to combine them. Add the butter and cream cheese and pulse about 12 times, just until the dough begins to clump together (butter pieces will still be visible). Turn the dough out onto a very lightly floured work surface and gather it together.

2. Divide into 2 disks and wrap each in plastic wrap. Refrigerate for at least 1 hour or up to 2 days. (If the dough is chilled until it is hard, let it stand at room temperature for about 10 minutes before rolling out.) The dough can also be frozen, overwrapped with aluminum foil, for up to 1 month. Defrost overnight in the refrigerator before using.

INDEX

Note: *Italicized* page references indicate photographs.

Lobster
    Rolls, 82–83
    Stockpot Clambake, 84–86

M

Main courses
    Corn Hotcakes with Blackberry Syrup, 89–90, *91*
    Fettuccine with Creamy Zucchini Sauce, 101–2
    Flank Steak with Manhattan Marinade, 67–68
    Giant Zucchini with Lamb Stuffing, 75–77
    Grilled Chicken with Rosemary White Barbecue
        Sauce, 60, *61–62*
    Grilled Eggplant and Tomato Sandwiches, 87–88
    Grilled Hot Dogs with Quick Chowchow, *72*, 73–74
    Grilled Pork Chops with Fresh Asian Plum Sauce,
        69–70, *71*
    Lobster Rolls, 82–83
    Ratatouille Lasagna, 98–100
    Risotto with Tomatoes, Basil, and Ricotta Salata, 107–8,
        109
    Soft-Shell Crab BLT Sandwiches, 79–81, *80*
    Spaghetti with Roasted Summer Vegetable Sauce,
        103–4
    Spaghetti with Shrimp and Arugula Pesto, *94*, 95–96
    Spanish Burgers with Romesco and Manchego Cheese,
        63–64, *65*
    Stockpot Clambake, 84–86
    Ziti with Sausage, Sweet Peppers, and Corn, 105–6
Melon. *See* Cantaloupe; Watermelon
Menus
    A Mediterranean-Style Supper, 100
    A Relaxed Breakfast with Friends, 10
    Summer Holiday Cookout, 62
    A Summertime Picnic, 88
Mint
    Syrup, 23
    Watermelon, and Tomato Salad, *40*, 41
    -Watermelon Daiquiris, Frozen, 23–24
Muffins, Blueberry, Melt-in-Your-Mouth, 136–37

N

Nectarine Clafoutis, *148*, 149–50
Nectarines, about, 153
Nuts
    Apricots with Goat Cheese and Hazelnuts, 2, *3*
    Arugula Pesto, 48
    Classic Basil Pesto, 47–48
    Plum Tart with Walnut Streusel Topping, 154–55
    Raspberry and Almond Scones, 156–57

O

Onion, Sweet, Creamy Dressing, Layered Salad with,
    37–38
Onions, sweet, varieties of, 39

P

Pasta
    Fettuccine with Creamy Zucchini Sauce, 101–2
    Orzo with Toasted Corn and Scallions, 117–18
    Ratatouille Lasagna, 98–100
    Spaghetti with Roasted Summer Vegetable Sauce,
        103–4
    Spaghetti with Shrimp and Arugula Pesto, *94*, 95–96
    Ziti with Sausage, Sweet Peppers, and Corn, 105–6
Peach(es)
    Donut, in Rosemary Syrup with Blackberries, 143–45,
        144
    Pie, Sour Cream, 151–52
    removing skin from, 153
    selecting and ripening, 153
    White, Bellini Freezes, *8*, 9–10
Pepper(s). *See also* Chile peppers
    Gazpacho-Style Bread Salad, 45–46
    Grilled Hot Dogs with Quick Chowchow, *72*, 73–74
    Grilled Vegetable Salad with Tomato Vinaigrette, 55–57
    grilling or broiling, 66
    Peperonata, 121–23, *122*
    Ratatouille Lasagna, 98–100
    Red, and Eggplant Dip, 21–22